Politics, Human Rights, and
What the Buddha Said About Life

Other Works by Venerable Master Hsing Yun:

Being Good
For All Living Beings
Humanistic Buddhism: A Blueprint for Life
Chan Heart, Chan Art
Humble Table, Wise Fare

Sutra Commentaries
The Rabbit's Horn
The Great Realizations
The Sutra of the Medicine Buddha

Politics, Human Rights, and What the Buddha Said About

Life

Venerable Master Hsing Yun

Translated by Robert H. Smitheram

Published by Buddha's Light Publishing, Los Angeles

© 2011 Buddha's Light Publishing

By Venerable Master Hsing Yun
Translated by Robert H. Smitheram
Edited by Nathan Michon and John Gill
Cover photograph by Chih-cheng Chang
Cover and book design by Wan Kah Ong and John Gill

Published by Buddha's Light Publishing
3456 S. Glenmark Drive,
Hacienda Heights, CA 91745, U.S.A.
Tel: (626) 923-5144
Fax: (626) 923-5145
E-mail: itc@blia.org
Website: www.blpusa.com

Printed in Taiwan.

Library of Congress Cataloging-in-Publication Data

Xingyun, da shi.
    Life / Venerable Master Hsing Yun.
        p. cm.
    At head of title: Politics, human rights, and what the Buddha said about life
    Edited version of several talks previously published separately in Chinese.
    ISBN 978-1-932293-46-3
1. Life–Religious aspects–Buddhism. I. Title. II. Title: Politics, human rights, and what the Buddha said about life.
    BQ9800.F6392X552 2011
    294.3'444–dc22
                    2010029365

Contents

Preface

Do not go upon what has been acquired by repeated hearing; nor upon tradition; nor upon rumor; nor upon what is in a scripture; nor upon surmise; nor upon an axiom; nor upon specious reasoning; nor upon a bias towards a notion that has been pondered over; nor upon another's seeming ability; nor upon the consideration, "The monk is our teacher." Kalamas, when you yourselves know: "These things are good; these things are not blamable; these things are praised by the wise; undertaken and observed, these things lead to benefit and happiness," enter on and abide in them.

— The Buddha, from the *Kalama Sutta*
Translated by Soma Thera

Buddhists are called to challenge all they hear, even the teachings of the Buddha. It is this spirit of free inquiry that leads to the most meaningful discoveries. The Buddha taught us to learn from everyone around us, though we must ultimately be our own teachers and learn from what we *experience* to be true. It is, in part, this process of free inquiry that has allowed the many permutations of Buddhism to arise and flourish.

Master Hsing Yun's name may not be familiar to most Buddhists in the West, though his influence reaches far beyond his home monastery in Taiwan, Fo Guang Shan. As part of a generation of

Buddhist reformers in Taiwan, Master Hsing Yun has revolution-
ized Chinese Buddhism.

He is the founder of Fo Guang Shan, a Taiwanese Buddhist
monastery with over two hundred branch temples around the world
throughout Asia, Europe, Africa, Australia, and the Americas, as
well as many associated charitable and educational institutions.
He has adapted popular media to propagate Buddhism, including
developing newspapers, magazines, songs, and even a television
station with its own studios. He established universities to better
train his monastics and provide an affordable education for the
public, as well as developing some of the best research resources
for Chinese Buddhism. He has supported the rights and equality of women, both within the monastic order and society, and
played a critical role in the Theravada ordination of women. He
stepped down as abbot of Fo Guang Shan to institute a democratic
system of governance in his temples in which all future abbots
would be elected by popular vote to their positions with term limits. Internationally, he has been critical in opening up China to
religion and has played a diplomatic role in improving relations
between China and Taiwan. His direct impact on East Asia and his
influence on other teachers has been enormous.

The present work is an edited compilation of several talks giv-
en by Master Hsing Yun with the intention of providing a single
volume that outlines the unique and significant elements of his
teachings, for he is not without his own views born from the process of free inquiry.

Master Hsing Yun calls his approach to Buddhist teaching and
practice "Humanistic Buddhism," a name which denotes a commitment to making Buddhism relevant to and integrated with the
daily lives of its adherents. His Dharma talks are characterized by

his efforts to make Buddhism accessible for as broad an audience as possible, but another critical part of his integration of Buddhism and life includes developing opinions on matters of social justice and public policy. Unlike some Buddhist teachers, Master Hsing Yun does not shy away from expressing these views. In fact, an essential part of Master Hsing Yun's thought is the innate importance of engagement—to be concerned with society and to participate in public life is a virtue in itself. While it is possible to debate the relative merits of any given political stance or social viewpoint, to be completely apathetic is seen as an unequivocal mistake.

For Master Hsing Yun, religion must engage society. Fo Guang Shan expends great effort and resources to foster education by building universities and schools and providing charity and assistance to the sick and needy. Yet throughout his teachings, Master Hsing Yun charges religion primarily with the task of improving social mores and values.

Master Hsing Yun's view on the interaction between religion and government is necessarily complex, as his belief in the responsibilities of religion is paired with a commitment to the democratic decision making process, including the separation of church and state. His political views defy attempts at easy categorization. For example, he is completely committed to democratic institutions, freedom, and human rights, while also strongly believing in the importance of social order and that freedom necessarily has its limits. He pushes for innovation in Buddhist institutions by making use of popular media and new technology, but these innovations are supported by a commitment to realizing the Buddha's ideals as preserved in the Buddhist sutras.

Life is about the intersection of Buddhism with the other noteworthy issues: society, human rights, race, politics, democracy, environmentalism, war, and our future. It is not meant to communicate the formal elements of Buddhist study, but instead reflects one Buddhist master's view on living life, and what is important. For those readers who are interested, an explanation of Buddhist terminology and the relevant elements of Chinese history are provided in a glossary. For the committed student of Buddhist studies, there is an index of quoted texts to ease the problems of navigating the English, Sanskrit, and Chinese name variants of important Buddhist sutras.

Ultimately, one should read *Life* for its focus: not what we get out of life, nor even the search for the meaning of life, but *the meaning we put into this life.* Our actions, our speech, our thoughts—the joys, the sorrows, the love—it's what we do, who we are, and what we intend that creates our lives and the meaning in them. We are the meaning of our lives and its up to us to decide the direction they take.

Master Hsing Yun encourages us to take the path of harmony, tolerance, respect, and courage—a path on which all people can grow and cultivate themselves together. For it is in this harmonious cooperation that we can all awaken to the true potential of life on this earth.

John Gill and Nathan Michon
Hacienda Heights, CA
August 2010

Acknowledgments

Like all of Buddha's Light Publishing's endeavors, this project benefited from the contributions of many people. We would like to thank Venerable Tzu Jung, the Chief Executive of the Fo Guang Shan International Translation Center (FGSITC), Venerble Hui Chi, Abbot of Hsi Lai Temple, and Venerable Yi Chao, Director of FGSITC for their support and leadership. Robert H. Smitheram provided the translation, Nathan Michon and John Gill collected and edited the texts, and Tom Manzo and Shujan Cheng proofread the manuscript and prepared it for publication. The book was designed by Wan Kah Ong, and Chih-cheng Chang provided the cover photographs. Our appreciation goes to everyone who supported this project from conception to completion.

I

Life

An Introduction

Life is the most precious thing in the world, for without it nothing else would have meaning. We can understand life both in broad and narrow terms. It is not only human beings who are alive, but animals, chirping birds, trees, blooming flowers, and each blade of grass is alive as well. The mountains, rivers, and plains of our world, as well as the sun, moon, and stars are all brimming with vitality. All of nature and the earth itself have life, just as we do. In Buddhism there is a well-known verse that goes like this:

> Flowing water speaks
>   the words of the Buddha;
> The mountain scene is none other
>   than his pure body.

Within the sound of a babbling brook the Buddha, the awakened one, is teaching us. The surrounding mountain layered in the green of its trees and flowers, as well as the entirety of the universe itself is the Buddha's *Dharmakaya*, the aspect of the Buddha that is present throughout all of existence. The Buddha is not different from the absolute reality of the universe, and the universe is not different from the Buddha. We each have a life, and each is equally precious beyond distinction. However, most people still lack a sense of inquiry and the desire to know more about life.

Life can be defined as that which can grow, and is active and functioning. With this definition, even the clothes on our backs have a life. If you cherish them, they can be worn for seven or eight years, but if you do not they can only be worn for three to five months before they are worn out. The same is true for a table, a chair, or a car; if I cherish it, I can use it for several decades, but if I do not, then these items will break and fall apart in just a few years.

Even time itself has a life. Our "lives" are our experiences accumulated over time, so wasting time is a form of taking life. Similarly, being casually wasteful is also taking life, because whatever the material object may be, it is a resource for all and came into existence with every other living thing serving as its causes and conditions. Therefore, not only do human beings have life, but all the things in the universe have life.

Our lives are also not limited to the time between birth and death. We can easily recognize and appreciate life as it is lived, but death too is a continuation of life. Death is actually just another stage of life. Death is not the end of everything; for death only means that one lifetime has ended, and another lifetime has begun, just as a clock moves its hands from one, to two, up to twelve, and then begins the cycle again. Life and death can be compared to planting a seed: a seed is planted in the ground and slowly sprouts, grows, and flowers, until it produces its own seeds which will grow into another new life.

Life and death are merely a part of a cycle, for according to Buddhism, life does not end. Death is just a link in a chain, a kind of metamorphosis marking the beginning of another lifetime. The fundamental essence of life is not altered in any way.

These questions of birth and death are only a part of what makes up life. Human beings must act to be vibrant and fully alive, and it is life itself that allows us to act. Consider our sense organs: when the eyes go blind you could say they have no "life" in them, and when the ears go deaf they lack this "life" as well. In the same way if we lose our sense of touch and the mind can no longer understand these sensations, how will it be able to show the energy of life? Once we have developed a sense of life's unlimited potential, we will then be able to see activity in the life of each member of our family, and how the life of every person in the community flourishes. As we move about the world, we will discover that all life is pulsating along with us. This energy of life must be present before any human life can become meaningful.

Though it can be said that we each have our own individual existence, life is not something that can be split apart. Each individual life coexists with every other life, such that all life is one. Life depends on many causes and conditions beings present, and the rising and falling of these causes and conditions is continuous and unending.

The purpose of life is to use our time to create these causes and conditions, called *karma*, for the lives that are to follow. We are only able to have our own lives because of the conditions and karmic connections from our country, community, parents, teachers, and friends. We should forge these same kinds of connections with others, so that they may have the same kinds of karmic opportunities we have had. We should create better karmic conditions and opportunities for our future lives, as well as contribute to the life of all humanity and the life of the *greater* self.

Life is an endless cycle of growth, and should exist through the qualities of truth, goodness, and beauty. When we help others to mature morally, deepen their faith, find opportunity at the workplace, and take a smoother path towards the future, then we are protecting life.

The bucolic joy of birds chirping, insects buzzing, birds flying, and fish swimming makes the world vibrant and colorful. Our daily lives are intimately connected with nature, for we cannot live without sunlight, air, and water. But nature not only brings forth life; it has a life of its own. Being alive does not just mean having breath, but that one functions and is useful. The mountains, rivers, and plains have purpose and everything that has use, has life. The chirping birds, buzzing insects, roaring waterfalls, and flowing springs with all their dazzling colors and verdant vibrancy are each signs of nature's flourishing growth that is teeming with life. Of all the phenomena throughout the vastness of the universe, which does not flow freely from our own life? We must therefore respect nature, care for it, and treasure it.

There is a famous letter attributed to Chief Seattle, a Native American who was negotiating with the United States government for the sale of his people's land. The letter reads:

> We are part of the earth and it is part of us. The perfumed flowers are our sisters, the bear, the deer, the great eagle, these are our brothers. The rocky crests, the juices in the meadow, ... and man, all belong to the same family ... the earth

does not belong to man, man belongs to the earth. All things are connected.

The letter has become an important statement for environmentalism, one that clearly and movingly demonstrates how the sky, earth, human beings, and all things form a living community. Human beings have unlimited potential, but they are not superior to nature. Humans beings must not only live peacefully with each other, but be able to peacefully coexist with nature. Some people say that animals are born to be eaten by human beings; this is an extraordinarily mistaken idea. In this world there is no one so great that he can absolutely rule over the many, and no one so strong that he can completely dominate the weak. Even though the lion is king of the jungle, he can still die of starvation if a thorn is stuck in his paw and he can no longer move about to find food.

Nature supports the existence of all of humanity and everything in the universe. How is it that we can damage and destroy it with such light consideration? Suppose for a moment that there was someone so warlike that he was able to conquer and kill all the people in the world. Who would now cook his food when he is hungry? Who would make clothes for him to wear? Human survival relies upon mutual interdependence. One person can only exist when others exist.

The whole world is interconnected. Consider lightning as an example: if there were no lightning, it would be impossible for plants to absorb nitrogen. About eighty percent of the earth's atmosphere is nitrogen, which is an essential nutrient for plants. The air above every square mile of land contains about twenty-two hundred tons of this nutrient. However, this gaseous nitrogen cannot be easily dissolved into water and so is completely useless for plants. It must undergo some process of change before plants can absorb it. It turns out that lightning can induce this kind of chemical change in nitrogen, transforming the gaseous form of nitrogen into something that plants are able to absorb. According to estimates, each year two billion tons of nitrogen fertilizer is produced over the surface of the earth through this conversion process.

This is but a single example, yet it skillfully shows how everything in the world exists through a web of mutual dependencies and interrelationships. We should cherish and protect nature, so that we can live peacefully with it. The earth is where we live, and we should take good care of it.

Earth's rivers, oceans, forests, mountains, and animals are just like the parts that make up the human body. The rivers are like the circulatory system, for their uninterrupted flow smoothly delivers nutrients. The oceans are like the kidneys, and it is by keeping them clean that we can maintain the planet's metabolism. The forests are like the heart and lungs; by reducing deforestation we can ensure that our air is well regulated. The mountains are like the skeleton; by reducing mining and excavation we can maintain the earth's climate. Animals are like the cells in the body; by not hunting and killing we can maintain a proper ecological balance. Only the long-term preservation of the earth's resources will guarantee humanity's long-term survival and a prosperous, happy life for future generations.

To exist, people must know how to be humble and peacefully get along with nature, and establish a relationship of oneness and coexistence. Life cannot exist without the web of causes and conditions upon which everything depends; the Buddha called this concept "dependent origination."

Dependent origination, as realized by the Buddha, explains how all phenomena arise and cease due to causes and conditions. All phenomena, both sentient and non-sentient, undergo the process of arising, ceasing, and change through a combination of causes and conditions. For example, each time we eat a meal, we must rely upon the tilling of the farmer, the marketing of the wholesaler, and the culinary efforts of the cook. Each article of clothing we wear is made possible through the hard work of so many people, from thread spinning and cloth making to tailoring and garment finishing. The houses we live in can protect us from the wind and rain only because of foresters planting trees, carpenters cutting wood, architects designing blueprints, and construction workers doing the building. Our daily needs of food, clothing, shelter, and transportation, as well as our recreation, all derive from the combined accomplishments of living beings in all directions. We should feel deeply thankful.

Generally speaking, most of humanity's misery comes from a failure to find harmony among the people, actions, things, and situations that are set in opposition to them. But by applying the Buddhist teachings and contemplating how these things arise due to causes, and are ultimately impermanent, we can face all of the arising, ceasing, and change of the universe.

By seeing how the earth itself teaches the Dharma through the rivers and trees, we can come to recognize our own intrinsic nature. When we understand our own intrinsic nature and know our true life, we can experience the enlightened state where there is no duality between the self and others, between the mundane and the supramundane, or between us and outside things. Our hearts and the world merge and become one.

If we can do this, then the flowers, grass, trees, mountains, and rivers of nature realize the perfection of wisdom together, and join us as we complete the Buddhist path. There is a Buddhist verse that goes:

> I see the charm and beauty
> of the green mountains,
> And consider that the mountains
> see me as such too.

When we can feel as openhearted as a fresh breeze or a clear moon, imagine how free and happy life can be.

II

Dharma

The Buddhist Worldview

The Buddha referred to his teachings as the *Dharma*, though this is a complex word with many definitions and no exact translation. At its most basic, Dharma means "truth." When used in a broad sense this can mean the truth of the universe, and describes reality as it really is.

To provide a complete understanding of the universe and human life is a task that is broad and requires a considerable amount of depth, touching upon principles extremely subtle and profound. It is not something that is easily explained in a few words.

In order to begin our own search for truth, it is good to start by understanding what truth is. In order for something to be true, it must meet four conditions: it must be fundamentally true, like saying that a square has four sides; it must be repeatable and true every time something occurs; it must be universally true in all places and for all people; and it must be true forever. In Buddhism, there are three maxims which conform to these four conditions for truth, and they are called the "three Dharma seals." The three Dharma seals are:

- All conditioned phenomena are impermanent.
- All phenomena are without an independent self.
- Nirvana is perfect tranquility.

The three Dharma seals explain the process of arising, abiding, change, and cessation that human life and the universe undergo, while also defining the liberated state of the Buddha. The three Dharma seals encompass all mundane and supramundane phenomena. All conditioned phenomena in the world arise from a combination of causes and conditions. These phenomena are empty of self-nature, for they arise as conditions come together and are extinguished when conditions disperse, while transiting endlessly through the past, present, and future.

All forms of life are born, grow old, get sick, and die; just as all features of the natural world, like mountains, rivers, and the planet earth itself go through formation, abiding, destruction, and cessation. Even thoughts go through arising, abiding, change, and extinction.

This world is governed by the eternal law of impermanence, which means that nothing remains unchanging forever. Actually, impermanence is a good thing because it gives significance to human life. It is because everything is impermanent and passes away that life and death are matters of supreme importance, and it is what necessitates that we practice diligently. It is because of impermanence that the cells in our body replicate and die in the metabolic process, which is how they maintain the body's vitality. There is an old Chinese saying:

> The waves behind push the waves in front
> down the Yangzi River;
> New people appear to replace the old
> within this human world.

New things emerging to replace what is outmoded is also impermanence, for it is only in this way that society as an organism can constantly manifest a youthful vitality through continuous renewal.

Impermanence is the true reality of the world. The *Diamond Sutra* says:

> All conditioned phenomena
> Are like dreams, illusions, bubbles, and shadows;
> Like dew and lightning.
> One should contemplate them in this way.

The *Treatise on the Perfection of Great Wisdom* states, "The world is impermanent; like the moon reflected in water or the brittle plantain tree. Merit enough to fill the three realms can be ruined by the winds of impermanence." Not only are fame and fortune like a dream at midnight, but even our precious bodies can only live for several decades or a hundred odd years at the very most. The world, our bodies, and even our thought processes all shift and change unceasingly. All things are mutable and insubstantial like clouds in the sky, froth upon the waves, images in a mirror, or the moon reflected in water. There is nothing that possesses any immutability or substantiality.

Non-self

Not only is everything in the world impermanent, but nothing possesses an "independent self." "Self" here is defined as an entity that is permanent and is able to exert agency. However, is there anything in the world that can act and exist in complete isolation from everything else? Of course not! All phenomena arise due to causes and conditions and cease due to causes and conditions. Nothing in this world can appear or exist without the necessary combination of causes and conditions, and once they disperse the thing itself ceases to be.

The Buddhist tradition has a parable about the self involving a traveler and two ghosts: One night a traveler realized he had long ago passed the inn he had intended to stay at. As it had already grown very dark, he decided to stay the night at the shrine of a local deity. As the night drew on, he was shocked to see a squat figure emerge, so ghastly it could only be described as a ghost, dragging a corpse behind him. The traveler was very frightened, but it was not long before a second, taller ghost lumbered by and shouted at the little ghost, "What are you doing? That's my corpse!"

The little ghost shouted, "It's mine! How dare you!"

The two ghosts continued to argue, while the traveler became so frightened he started to tremble, and caught the attention of the little ghost.

"There's a man under the altar," the little ghost said, "Come out of there, don't be afraid. You must have seen the whole thing. Tell us, who does this corpse belong to?"

The traveler thought for a moment, and realized there was no getting out of this situation, so he decided to simply answer honestly.

"The corpse belongs to the shorter ghost."

The moment he heard this, the larger ghost became incensed and lunged at the traveler, snapped off his right arm, and gobbled it up in two bites. The little ghost felt as though he could not stand by and do nothing since the traveler had vouched for him, so he ripped the right arm off the corpse and stuck it on to the traveler's body.

Still angry, the large ghost ripped off the traveler's left arm and devoured it as well, which the little ghost quickly replaced with the corpse's arm. The large ghost continued to eat away at the traveler, until the small ghost had replaced all of the traveler's limbs. After they were done toying with the traveler, both ghosts left, leaving the traveler to look down upon his body, confused.

"Who am I?" the traveler gasped.

This story may make its point in a gruesome way, but it is meant to teach us that this body does not belong to us. Rather, it exists as an impermanent combination of the four great elements of earth, water, fire, and wind. The bodies of all living beings are formed through a combination of these elements. For example, the "earth element" encompasses things which are hard and solid, including the hair, nails, teeth, skin, flesh, muscles, and bones of the human body. Mucus, saliva, pus, blood, phlegm, tears, and urine are the "water element," which encompasses anything liquid or fluid. The "fire element" encompasses the heat generated by the body, and the "wind element" encompasses the breath as it enters and leaves the body.

Human beings can only exist because of the combination of these four elements of physicality, liquidity, heat, and movement. If there is an imbalance among any of the four great elements, the body will become sick.

Everything can be analyzed in terms of the four great elements. For example, if a flower is to blossom, the earth element must be present in the form of soil and there must also be moisture, sunlight, and air, which are the water, fire, and air elements, respectively. If any one of these elements is missing, then the flower cannot fully bloom.

SUFFERING

Buddhism teaches that suffering is one of the truths of human life, and that understanding it is the first step toward a life free from suffering. There is a saying in Buddhism:

> A time will come when
>   both heaven and hell will end,
> Yet suffering in the human realm
>   will never, ever cease.

When you and I do not get along, that is suffering. When you lack money, material possessions, or love; that is suffering. When you cannot get rid of people you dislike, that is suffering. When the body experiences old age, sickness, and death, that is suffering. When you experience greed, hatred, delusion, ignorance, or hold wrong views, that is suffering. The deceptions, kidnappings, and injustices that occur in society are suffering. The criticism of others and the vagaries of right or wrong, success or failure, and praise or blame are suffering. Fighting, war, and oppression are suffering. Earthquakes, typhoons, fires, floods, and other natural disasters are suffering.

Where does pain and suffering come from? It comes from the "I." "I" am the source of desire, "I" am greedy, and "I" am selfish.

When we only think about ourselves, there is suffering. In this way, suffering comes from our karma.

KARMA

A simple way to explain karma is to say "Good is rewarded with good, and bad is repaid with bad." Karma is experiencing the consequences of your own actions. No one else can experience the results of our own karma, for it falls to us.

Once there was a child whose mother always took care of things for him. When he was doing homework, his mom would say, "You go to sleep, Mom will do it for you." or "You go watch TV, Mom will do your composition." One time, the child was careless and cut his hand with a knife. He screamed, "It hurts! It hurts! Mom, please take the pain away for me!"

But this is not how the world works, and there are many things for which other people are unable to take your place. Whether we experience happiness or suffering is created by each one of us through our karma.

Any given thing in the world has its causes and effects, but these causes and effects can be very complicated. Causes can be positive or negative, while karmic effects can also be positive or negative depending upon which of these qualities is more pronounced. Consider the example of a field: there will be some seeds that do not grow well, while others will grow healthy and strong without any differences in the conditions met by the two kinds of seeds. Differences in the constituent causes of a phenomena lead to different karmic effects.

Karma is the result of our actions, including what we say, what we think, and what we do. These are known as the "three karmas."

Karma can also be divided into "positive karma" and "negative karma." When the karma we have created reaches fruition, we will experience its effects, positive or negative, in accordance with what we have done. Karmic power controls our future without the slightest error.

Karma can be categorized in many other ways. For example, what influences a single individual is generally called "specific karma," while what affects a group is called "collective karma." For example, all those who are born in Taiwan share the collective karma that leads them to be born there. All living beings share some collective karma, regardless of whether they are born in Asia, Europe, or Africa, or whether their skin is yellow, white, brown, or black.

Buddhism speaks of causality as the true reality of human life in the universe. The causality that Buddhism articulates is not just about encouraging people to do good, nor does it merely represent a branch of theoretical knowledge for study. All aspects of life have their causal relationships—the clothes, food, rest, and activities within our daily lives, as well as how we get along with others, our faith, morality, health, and finances. Nothing is outside the web of cause and effect. For example, eating can relieve the pangs of hunger; eating is the cause, while the satisfied feeling of fullness is the effect. Then there is the case of someone who works diligently and makes a lot of money. Here, working hard is the cause, while making money is the effect.

Causality is a most profound philosophy. The law of karma states that every cause has an effect. Karma is beyond the control of humans and cannot be changed by heaven or supernatural beings. Karma governs human life and everything in the universe, for it plants the causes and conditions across the past, present, and future. The "Bequeathed Teachings" chapter in the *Mahaparinirvana Sutra* indicates the gravity of the situation:

> Positive effects for good and negative effects for bad follow each other like a shadow after its form; cause and effect of the past, present, and future revolve in their cycle and are never lost. It is too late to regret once a life has been spent in vain.

Everything comes from karma: an individual's fortune or misfortune, poverty or wealth, and honor or ignominy. Even the length of your life and the beauty of your appearance arise from cause and effect relationships; they do not simply appear out of nowhere. The poem "The Ten Results and Their Causes" explains this profound idea in simple terms:

> Pleasing looks come from enduring disgrace;
> Poverty comes from stinginess and greed;
> High social rank comes from religious practice;
> Low and mean status comes from arrogance
> and pride;
> Muteness comes from slandering others;
> Blindness and deafness come from a lack of faith;
> Longevity comes from loving kindness
> and compassion;
> A short life comes from killing;
> Weakened faculties come from breaking
> the precepts;
> Strong faculties come from observing
> the precepts.

Many Buddhists misunderstand cause and effect, and have unreasonable expectations. For example, some people believe that just by maintaining a vegetarian diet they can live a long life, or that by simply paying homage to a Buddha statue they will get a promotion or become rich. These actions come from an incorrect view of causality. It is true that things like faith, morality, health, and wealth are subject to cause and effect, but one must always consider the whole picture. If you want to be healthy not only should you maintain a balanced mind and do good deeds, but you must exercise and pay attention to your health. If you want to be rich you should create positive karmic connections with others, work hard, keep your promises, and cultivate wisdom.

The *Lotus Sutra* emphasizes that we all have both positive and negative karma. Even so, as long as we cultivate more positive karma, the minor offenses will not have that big of an impact. In the same way, if both weeds and grain seedlings are growing in a field, as long as you preserve and slowly remove the weeds, by the time the grain has grown tall these weeds will no longer affect the harvest.

As long as we take Buddhism's compassion and wisdom to heart, then we will naturally create positive karma. There is a saying in Buddhism, "One dispels darkness with light, and one obtains peace and security with the Dharma."

PRECEPTS

One of the fundamental ways of dispelling negative karma and producing positive karma is through the observance of moral precepts. The basic set of precepts that Buddhism advocates are known as the "five precepts." The five precepts are:

1. To refrain from killing.
2. To refrain from stealing.
3. To refrain from sexual misconduct.
4. To refrain from lying.
5. To refrain from consuming intoxicants.

An element that these five precepts have in common is that they ask us to be respectful and not violate the rights of others. For example, to refrain from killing is to not violate others' right to life. To refrain from stealing is to not violate others' right to property. To refrain from sexual misconduct means not violating others' right to their own body. To refrain from lying is to not violate the reputation of others. To refrain from consuming intoxicants is preserving our wisdom so that we will not violate our own rights or the rights of others.

If everyone could accept and practice the five precepts not only would the prisons be empty, but as each of us practice we would improve our moral character. If an entire family were to practice the five precepts, that would mean an improvement of the character of that family, and so on for any group, community, or country. If we could all practice the five precepts, society would be harmonious and stable. By propagating the Buddha's teachings and practicing the five precepts the mores of society and our collective karma will naturally improve.

Respect for Life

In Chinese, there is a saying that "Heaven's virtue is its care for living things." Buddhism is a religion that is infused with compassion; and the compassion to not kill living beings is something which all

Buddhists should observe. The *Treatise on the Perfection of Great Wisdom* says:

> Among all forms of wrongdoing,
>   the guilt of killing is the most serious.
> Among all virtues,
>   not killing is foremost.

As can be seen in the first precept, Buddhism has a profound respect for life. In Buddhism everything from killing a human being to killing cockroaches, mice, mosquitoes, and ants is considered taking life. "Taking life" encompasses those situations where a life is ended, including killing yourself, teaching others how to kill, and approving of killing. Some people kill with tangible weapons, while others use intangible means, like words, to harm their victims. Destroying another's hope, spreading rumors, and crushing another's confidence are all forms of taking life. When we harm through our actions, speech, or thoughts, we are taking life.

In the Buddhist monastic rules, the offenses related to taking life are divided into two groups. One group of violations is called *duskrta*, which includes slight misdeeds, while another category, *parajika*, covers more grave offenses. *Parajika* rules leave no room for redemption, and those monastics who violate them are expelled from the monastic order. Only murdering a human being is considered a *parajika* offense. The killing of cockroaches, ants, and other insects is a *duskrta* offense. This is still a form of wrongdoing, and is a violation of the precepts, but Buddhism does not hold it in the same regard as killing a human being. Those who commit *duskrta* offenses may repent for what they have done, and counteract their transgression by performing good deeds. For example, some people set caged animals free to amend for their offenses, while others undergo repentance ceremonies or make vows as a way to ameliorate their negative karma.

While Buddhism asks its followers not to kill, to go through life without killing anything is not all that easy. We transgress the precept against killing every day, and we destroy many non-human beings without even realizing it. For example, if you go to the doctor and receive an injection that kills the bacteria in your body, is this not taking life? The sutras say that "When the Buddha gazes upon a glass of water, he sees eighty-four thousand beings." If you were to then drink this water, wouldn't it be taking life? When the body of a dead person is cremated, even if the person has passed away the body still contains many living cells and microorganisms. When the body is burned, is this not taking life?

Such unconscious misdeeds are only slightly negative, for what is most important is that we do not take life with the intent to kill, or under the influence of anger or hatred. As we develop our Buddhist practice there may be instances when we kill, but it is important not to generate the negative mental karma of killing living beings. Even if our actions thoughtlessly harm or kill small organisms, we can repent and make amends for it.

The effects of karma do not only depend on how we act, but are also influenced by our motivations. If we violate one of the precepts, the karmic effect will be different if we have good intentions, bad intentions, or no intention at all. The Venerable Daoxuan, a master of the monastic rules, said:

> Killing an ant with an intention to do harm is more serious than killing a person with a compassionate motivation. Such karma is inherently serious and

it is that which determines the karmic retribution received. Even though one repents such grave offenses, the karmic process is not eliminated.

The Buddhist analysis of karma recognizes different degrees of severity depending on the type of wrongdoing. The negative karmic effects of those who take pleasure in killing, or who kill for revenge, is much more severe when compared to those who kill out of self-defense or simply to survive. This is similar to our legal system, which recognizes differences in the severity of punishment depending upon the nature of the crime, whether it be homicide, premeditated murder, impulse murder, murder as a crime of passion, involuntary manslaughter, or murder committed while intoxicated.

The Buddhist code of conduct is not a perilous path to follow, nor does it tie down our freedom. We should not think that the Buddhist precepts are too severe, and that they are impossible to obey. The Buddhist precepts are endowed with the spirit of freedom and tolerance, and through observing them we learn that an even greater freedom comes from not violating the freedom of others.

BUDDHISM IN THE WORLD

Many people believe that Buddhism should engage in social service, and may even define Buddhism by its charity work. But this is not the most important task of a religion. Anyone can provide relief, and any group or organization can engage in charity work. However, religious groups are uniquely charged with purifying the mind, and improving social mores. Buddhism in particular should undertake such duties.

The problems of society are everyone's problems, and they demand the united care and concern of all people. No matter how bad the problems in this world may become, as long as we can summon everyone's thoughtful consideration these problems can be reduced. Some can even be eliminated.

Buddhism is a religion which aims to combine moral behavior *and* knowledge. Buddhism does not de-emphasize the importance of knowledge, for it is important. However, most people would agree that the purpose of knowledge and scholarship is to allow us to better adapt to the world we live in. Yet scholars and other highly knowledgeable people do not necessarily live happy lives. Any branch of science, philosophy, or literature which leads us to better understand the world is still only a derivative form of knowledge, rather than direct understanding. Worldly knowledge is "impure learning," while the Dharma is undefiled learning. Worldly knowledge brings with it a mixture of both benefit and harm. Buddhist knowledge, called *prajna* wisdom, is knowledge that arises from removing all selfishness from the mind. The goal of Buddhism is to remove our delusion and develop the *prajna* wisdom that lies within ourselves.

In Buddhist terms, whatever prevents us from understanding the true nature of the cycle of birth and death is delusion. Delusion is not the total lack of knowledge. In Chinese, the character for "delusion" is *chi* (痴), which is made up of two components. The center of the character is the same as *zhi* (知), the character for knowledge, with the addition of the radical *chuang* (疒), meaning

sickness. Delusion, instead of the absence of knowledge, is knowledge that has something wrong with it.

Delusion obscures the true nature of the mind and the world
around us. Delusion is what keeps us from liberation and causes
us to generate karma, be reborn in the cycle of birth and death,
and experience the suffering contained therein. However, immediately after the Buddha's awakening, he made the following
proclamation:

> "Marvelous, marvelous! All sentient beings have
> the Tathagata's* wisdom and virtue, but they fail
> to realize it because they cling to deluded thoughts
> and attachments."

In Buddhism, this is known as the declaration of Buddha nature: the assertion that all living beings innately possess the wisdom to become Buddhas. Just as the brightness of the sun may
be obscured by clouds, it is only because our Buddha nature is
obscured by our afflictions and delusion that we fail to recognize
this. It is because our Buddha nature is obscured that we have
sorrow and suffering, and continue to be reborn within the cycle
of birth and death. The failings of human life, all of the conflict,
discord, discrimination, and disappointments are present because
of a failure to realize our own Buddha nature.

Buddhism teaches that *all* living beings have Buddha nature.
Since everyone possesses the potential to become a Buddha, why
would we ever belittle ourselves unfairly, or treat ourselves as if
we were insignificant? That is why I feel that everyone should live
with dignity and know that they are no different from the Buddha.

* *Tathagata* is another name for the Buddha, and the one he most
frequently used when talking about himself.

An ordinary person is simply a Buddha that has not yet awakened, and a Buddha is just an ordinary person who has. Everyone innately has Buddha nature, and not a single living being lacks it. That is why, when conducting ceremonies, I encourage everyone to remember the phrase "I am a Buddha." If we acknowledge and take on the responsibility of each of us being a Buddha, then we can hold our heads high without fear or shame, and join with the Buddha.

When we learn about Buddhism and practice its teachings, we wipe away the dust that obscures our Buddha nature, allowing the mind to become bright and things to be revealed just as they are. In this way we can be liberated and realize a state of perfect freedom that is beyond birth and death and that has transcended the notion of a separate self and the limitations of time and space. This is the ultimate goal of Buddhist learning and practice. To reach this goal, Buddhists undertake what is called the "threefold training," which is the cultivation of morality, meditative concentration, and wisdom. By undertaking the threefold training we are able to eliminate our greed, hatred, and delusion, and attain the blissful state of freedom.

THE PURE LAND

Throughout the Buddhist sutras various realms called "Pure Lands" are mentioned. A Pure Land is a transcendent realm created through the power of a Buddha's vow to help ease the suffering of living beings, should they choose to be reborn there. The sutras mention many different Pure Lands, including Maitreya Bodhisattva's Pure Land, Amitabha Buddha's Pure Land, the Medicine Buddha's Pure Land, the Flower Adornment Pure Land, Vimalakirti's Pure Land,

and many others. Each Pure land is unique and possesses its own special qualities.

Due to the scientific and technological advances of our modern world, we see some aspects of the Pure Lands in our human realm. For example, the Medicine Buddha's Pure Land is described as having abundant food and clothing, lodging and transportation available to all, and medicine available to anyone who needs it. Beings in the Medicine Buddha's Pure Land live without trouble, and this is not too different from the lives of many people in developed countries. The goal of Humanistic Buddhism is to merge together the qualities of the various Pure Lands to create a Pure Land here on earth for all living beings.

The Pure Land of Humanistic Buddhism is this very world transformed by Buddhism. In such a Pure Land people take refuge in the Triple Gem, observe the five precepts, understand cause and effect, and forge positive karmic connections with others. In such a world all that we see are beautiful things, all that we hear are pleasant sounds, all that we say are fine words, and all that we do are good deeds. There will no longer be jealousy among people, only mutual respect. Hatred will be absent, and all that remains will be harmony. Instead of greed, everyone will give to one another joyfully. A Humanistic Buddhist Pure Land is a world of bliss, where everyone strolls amid the pleasant warmth of spring winds and each family is bathed in the compassionate light of the Dharma. Any time is a good time, and every place is a world of *prajna.*

To build this Pure Land we must spread Humanistic Buddhism, and ensure that the Buddha's teachings are implemented and become a part of daily life. When the Dharma is embedded in the heart of each individual, then the Buddha will be present in everyone's heart. We will see the world as the Buddha sees it, hear the voice of the Buddha in each sound, speak only the Buddha's words, and think only with the Buddha's kindness. When the body and mind are purified, the Pure Land will appear at that very moment. Then people can live a life transformed by Buddhism, a life that is liberated and free. To build this world, we each need to work towards it. Thus it is my hope that we can all band together to build this Pure Land.

III

The Cycle of Life

In principle, living in an age of advanced technology and material abundance should mean that people live a happy life. However, more and more people feel unhappy and lack a sense of peace and stability. If this psychological quandary is not resolved, there will be no end to our societal problems.

We are facing a variety of social problems at present, including a warping of our values, the degradation of social standards, the collapse of morality, an unfair and biased media, the erosion of human rights, the impotence of justice, the silencing of truth, and a lack of moral courage. All of these problems stem from an illness of the spirit. This problem more than any other needs to be solved, and we must begin by looking at the mind throughout the stages of life.

Each one of us should make a plan for our life. Confucius had his own career plan:

> At fifteen I set my mind to learning; at thirty, I was established; at forty, I no longer had doubts;

at fifty, I knew the will of heaven; at sixty, nothing
I heard upset me; and at seventy, I can follow
my heart's desire without transgressing what is
right.

I too once mapped out my own life, with each decade dedicated to something different. The first ten years were my period of
growing up, the second were a period of learning, followed by a
decade of acquiring knowledge, a decade dedicated to literature, a
decade of philosophy, a decade of history, a decade to understand
ethical principles, and a decade for teaching Buddhism. Having
lived through these eight periods, in the end they have all returned
to Buddhism, for it is in the single truth of the dharma realm that
life is perfected.

MAKING A LIVING

Buddhism teaches what it calls the Noble Eightfold Path. One
of the eight factors of the path is called "right livelihood," which
means earning an income and making a living in a proper way. The
29th chapter of the *Treatise on the Stages of Yogacara Practitioners*
defines right livelihood as follows:

To seek clothing, food, and even miscellaneous
goods according to the Dharma, so that one turns
away from all perverse forms of making a living,
is known as right livelihood.

Having a proper way to make a living is extremely important for individuals, families, and the community. This is because a

large part of the world's ills stem from wrong forms of livelihood. Some examples include establishing gambling dens, bars, criminal money lending operations, and slaughter houses, or operating stores that sell fishing tackle, hunting rifles, and the like. None of these constitute right livelihood.

Besides providing the necessities of life, work can actually be our best form of practice by allowing us to make donations, provide service, and connect with others. Thus, while it is important for us to engage in right livelihood, while on the job we should also possess good professional ethics:

1. We must be mindful of karma.
Do not take advantage of your station and engage in corruption, commit fraud, seek private gain at the public's expense, profit from forced seizures, or benefit from intimidation or enticements. Everything that is gained should be returned to the public in total.

2. We must be patient.
Do not complain when tasked with responsibilities, nor blame others when difficulties arise. Work hard without complaint, for everything should be seen as a matter of course. Patience is what allows us to do our jobs and take on their responsibilities.

3. We must work conscientiously.
Bear responsibilities earnestly and take pleasure in doing so. If problems arise do not shift them to others, for you should not enjoy abusing other people. Make things easier for others and serve them. This is what it means to work conscientiously.

4. *We must be grateful.*

Be grateful for everything. Be thankful that the boss has given you a job, and be thankful that your coworkers and subordinates have assisted your work. As long as you have a grateful heart you can do things happily, no matter how busy or tired you may be.

Once there was a company that was hiring and a talented student who had graduated from Tokyo University went to be interviewed. Before the interview, the company president asked him, "Have you helped dry your father and mother off after a bath? Have you massaged their backs?"

The young man replied, "I did when I was younger, but haven't done so since."

The president said, "Alright. First I want you to go back and dry them off and massage their backs. Then come back tomorrow for the interview."

The young man's father had passed away long ago, and his mother worked every day to earn money so that he could study. He normally did not see his mother that much, so he had no idea how he could go to her now and ask if he could dry her back. When his mother returned home that night he said to her, "Mom, let me wash your feet for you."

His mother was quite surprised and asked, "How come you suddenly think of washing my feet today?"

The young man replied, "The president of the company where I'm seeking employment told me that I must serve you first."

"Oh, if that's what you need to do, then okay. You may wash my feet for me."

As the young man washed his mother's feet, he saw that they were heavily calloused, and there were even some chapped sores from frostbite. He began to feel quite upset, for he realized that the money his mother had made to provide for his schooling had come through her toil and sweat, at the expense of her own health.

The next day, the young man returned to the company to see the president and said, "Boss, I have not come here today to ask for a job; I simply want to thank you. It's because you told me to go home and serve my mother that I have been able to learn the most precious lesson in my life. This will serve me well for the rest of my life, and that is enough for me. I no longer care that you won't be selecting me for the job."

The president said, "You're hired. Now, let's get to work!"

FAMILY AND MARRIAGE

The family is the basic unit of society and marriage is the foundation for organizing the family. Having undergone the usual public ceremony for getting married, a man and woman are joined together as husband and wife and develop their family life from then on. This marks the beginning of human relationships.

Marriage is one of life's major events. Chinese culture in particular has thought that men and women should wed, simply as a matter of course. But with the growing openness of social customs as well as the influence of factors like the growing prominence of feminism, people today not only divorce at higher rates, but some people commit to being single their whole lives and never get married.

There are some people who would still like to be married, but they have doubts and worry about problems that may arise in the future, or whether or not their partner is right for them. In such cases many couples try to live together first as a sort of "trial marriage," but if there is a lack of faith in the marriage it only makes it easier to abandon the commitment as soon as problems arise. If a couple is unable to shoulder any responsibilities it will only create more problems.

Seeing marriage as a game is a very unwise attitude. For example, if a couple has a child, but they are only living together, do they separate if they feel they are not compatible? Once the next generation appears, the couple must shoulder the responsibilities that go along with having a child. That is why, in a marriage, a couple should consider these responsibilities from the outset. A couple should have faith in their commitment and plan for ways to build a healthy family. If they do not, they should not live together so casually.

When in love, many people have beautiful visions of marriage, and see marriage as marking the beginning of a happy family. But there are also those who say that marriage is the tomb of love. Indeed, how a husband and wife live together after a marriage and how to keep love from fading away truly make up a field of learning in its own right. Most marriages begin with so much attentiveness, trust, and understanding; and these feelings must be maintained throughout the marriage.

Getting married should not be like entering a tomb and allowing love to die. A marriage must be nurtured with great care, like a flower that must be watered so that it can bloom more fragrantly and beautifully. This is not the responsibility of just one person, for the couple must build this love together. Since marriage is the joining of two families, not just two individuals, there are many practical problems that need to be addressed. For example, after a couple is married there is not only one set of parents that must be looked after, but two. In a marriage it is not only the husband

and wife that must live together in mutual respect, understanding, and tolerance, but this same treatment must be extended to every member of the family, especially between the daughter-in-law and mother-in-law.

It is important that we think of others and treat them well. We should have the attitude that "You can be right, for I will be wrong; you may be great, for I will be small; you may have this, for I will do without; you may be happy, and I will take on hardship." With this attitude everyone, be it one family or two, can live together with joy and harmony. As human beings, we must watch out for selfishness. If you only think of yourself all the time and forget that others exist, then even the most loving couples will lose their affection in time, and the best of partners will find it difficult to live together. This is why the relationship between a husband and wife must be based on mutual respect. Mencius, one of the great Confucian philosophers, said, "He who respects others will be respected by them; and he who loves others will be loved by them." Only a respectful and loving marriage will last.

EDUCATING THE YOUNG

Education is the means by which humanity passes on and develops culture. There is a need for education, whether it is acquired at home, in school, or through society; but education is not merely a matter of passing on knowledge, for there is moral education, cognitive education, life education, and so on. One can only become knowledgeable and develop proper behavior through education. Thus I believe that everyone has the right and duty to receive a national education, and that parents and teachers must also bear the responsibility to educate their children and students.

Education must be applied with both leniency and strictness and exert both compassion and authority. This is similar to the experience of visiting a Chinese Buddhist temple: when you first enter the main gate of a traditional Chinese temple you are greeted by the plump visage of Maitreya, the happy Buddha, who accepts you with the smiling face of compassion. This symbolizes how we should use loving care to receive all living beings. But as one continues past the image of Maitreya, one will see the image of Skanda, a stern and awe-inspiring general armed with a *vajra* club for subduing demons. Buddhism receives you with compassion, trying as much as possible to give you joy and contentment. However, sometimes we also need a stern attitude to keep ourselves on a straight moral path. Likewise, in a family the children need both stern education and loving care. Compliance through sternness and acceptance through compassion are both equally important. The text, *Precious Teachings of the Chan Masters* says:

> Mother them with care, this is how
> spring and summer give birth to things.
> Temper them with frost and snow, this is how
> autumn and winter bring things to fruition.

Everything from caring for nature to educating the family requires both loving acceptance and assertive compliance. Thus parents and teachers cannot be too indulgent when it comes to the education of the next generation, but neither should they cause harm. When raising children in particular, one must protect their dignity, and not apply physical punishment too frequently. Appropriate physical punishments can sometimes be an effective form of instruction. But, strictly speaking, only those who lack an understanding of pedagogy employ physical punishments as a teaching method. The ideal form of education replaces reprimands with encouragement and substitutes critiques of the negative with praise for the good. This way children can grow up happy and positive in a healthy environment. Only then will the next generation have good character.

A person must have a sense of honor, for with it, one naturally seeks to better himself and will be drawn to what is good. Personally, I have always felt that an education which is based on beating and scolding will only make the students fearful and withdrawn. Students who perform poorly should be coached according to their capacity. For those students who are more obstinate in nature, one must provide loving instruction. No one has ever become intelligent through beating and scolding.

In handling problems, some teachers impose punishments before the facts of the matter are clearly ascertained, and may even punish an entire group or class. This kind of punishment can easily make the students unbalanced and uneasy. One must think carefully when it comes to methods of punishment, because you do not want to damage the students' self-esteem. We must supply them with encouragement to help them do better, ensuring that the supply of loving support and assertive compliance complement one another. This is the best kind of pedagogy.

In his *Analects*, Confucius says:

> If the people are governed by decree and kept in
> order by applying punishments, then they will
> stay out of trouble but have no sense of shame;
> if they are governed through virtue and kept in

order by the rules of propriety, then they will have
a sense of shame and *self*-reform.

In this world, most people's greatest desire is just to live a good and happy life. But the children in many families end up being unhappy due to the acrimony between parents or poor parenting itself. This is why they will develop themselves outwardly, hoping to find some source of happiness and excitement on the outside. In particular, most young people pursue romantic love with wholehearted intensity, and yet love is often fickle. Any storm that occurs in a romance can easily lead to depression if one lacks the strength to withstand it. Some will become pessimistic and dispirited, fall into despair, and may even contemplate suicide.

I once met a young man who had just suffered a failed romance and was preparing to commit suicide by jumping into a river. After I pulled him away, I asked him: "Why do you want to commit suicide?"

"Because I lost her!" he said

I told him, "We can see millions of stars in the sky, and there are more people on earth than the stars we see! Why kill yourself for just that one alone?"

Each of us have parents, siblings, and friends, so why do we torment ourselves over just one person? Young people will often get wrapped up in something and become stuck, and it is the parents and teachers who should provide them with the education during their childhood and adolescence that can protect them. Young people will then know how things can change from moment to moment—that "impermanence" may happen at any time.

THE AMBITIONS OF YOUTH

In Buddhism it is said that there are five main things we desire: wealth, sex, fame, food, and sleep. But which of these five desires would you say is the greatest? It is impossible to come to any final conclusion. However, what we can know is that trying to satisfy the limitless desires of humanity with the limitations of the material world is impossible. Twenty years ago, everyone in Mainland China dreamt of owning a bicycle, but after China opened to the outside world a bicycle was unable to satisfy people's desires. People then wished for motorbikes, but once someone owned a motorbike came the hope for a small automobile.

Now, would having a car bring satisfaction? No. As soon as one person saw another driving an imported car, they would begin to think of how grand it would be if they had one too. But would an imported car truly make anyone happy? Not when someone mentions they have a private plane. Trying to pursue happiness through material things will never lead to any satisfaction. I think life's greatest wealth is knowing how to be content, knowing how to be reasonable, and understanding the law of karma. Happiness comes from making do with what you have, and going without what you do not have. Do not blindly chase after meaningless things.

Young people today seem to have the power to summon the wind and bring down the rain, so why do they feel depressed? Any analysis of depression cannot rule out biological factors, but the majority of cases are a result of an unhealthy mind. Examples of such unhealthy mental states include paranoia, jealously, being unable to accept the success of others, comparing oneself with others, close-mindedness, an inability to think things through, aloofness, extremism, obsession, and so on. Such mental states can very easily lead to serious psychological problems.

These days people suffer from depression not as a result of life's pressures being too great, but because they are unwilling to accept life's challenges and stand up to its various trials. This is particularly true for those who hope to become famous overnight. Once their dreams are thwarted, they feel absolutely defeated. They may then react against such unfairness by resenting the world, and this leads to depression. The pervasiveness of depression today is related to the affluent and peaceful standard of living that most people have. Since they lack the strength of character that comes from suffering hardships and setbacks, they are unable to withstand a large amount of pressure. This is why I believe today's parents must help their children to develop moral courage from an early age to accept the tests of adversity though suffering hardships and setbacks. It is only in this way that young people can learn to bounce back.

THE ELDERLY

According to the World Health Organization, when the number of people over the age of sixty-five makes up more than seven percent of a country's population, that country is an "aging society." When those over sixty-five make up more than fourteen percent of the population, then the country is an "aged society." But whenever we speak of senior citizens, we must remember that the elderly are a treasure. Though the elderly may see a decline in their strength and eyesight, they possess a richness of life experience. They can serve as models for later generations to emulate, and their wisdom and experience can be passed on to posterity. There is a Chinese saying that, "To have an elderly person in your home is like possessing a precious jewel." The value of the elderly should not be taken lightly.

The Buddhist sutras contain a story about a country that had abandoned its elderly. The king in this country believed that old people only consumed the country's resources without contributing anything worthwhile, so he issued an edict making it illegal to keep the elderly in one's home, and thus drove all the elderly out of the country. Any family found harboring an old person would be punished severely. However, one of the king's ministers could not bear abandoning his aged father, so he secretly hid his father in the cellar. One day, a rival kingdom issued a challenge to the king in the form of a riddle, but no one was able to understand what the riddle meant. The king publicly proclaimed that anyone who could understand the challenge would be richly rewarded. No one had any idea how to solve the riddle, until the king's minister secretly asked his elderly father, who was able to answer it correctly. The rival kingdom submitted more challenges, and each time the minister's father secretly supplied his son with the answer. When the king asked his minister how he was able to answer the riddles, the minister revealed his father as the true source of his wise responses. Only then did the king realize that the elderly are neither a burden nor a nuisance; They are the country's treasure.

I read an article on the internet not long ago with the headline, "Obasans Save Taiwan." "Obasan" is an expression that essentially means "old lady." The article tells the story of a young student who forgot her lunchbox on the bus while she was hurriedly getting off at her stop. The other young people on the bus saw her lunchbox, and maybe muttered some muted gasps, but were too embarrassed to take any action. There was an old lady on the bus who saw the lunchbox too, but she was not embarrassed at all. She did not care what others would think, so she yelled out, "Miss! Your lunchbox!"

In Taiwan people do not often express themselves this way, especially on public transportation, so naturally her words drew glances from everyone. But she did not care. She kept calling out, "Miss! Your lunchbox!" Of course, no one else did much of anything, and the girl kept on walking away.

Just then, another old lady across the street became concerned, and shouted, "Hey! What are you saying?"

The old lady on the bus replied, "This lunchbox, it's hers!" she said, indicating the girl who was rushing away.

The old lady on the street then ran over, took the lunchbox from the old lady on the bus, and ran back across the street in pursuit of the child.

What we can learn from this story is that old ladies are sometimes more loving and caring towards society than young people. Thus, as people grow older, especially those who have retired, they must have faith in themselves and ensure that the older they become, the more enthusiastic and spirited they will be. They must come up with ways to create a second springtime in their lives. To do this the elderly can organize social clubs to make friends and interact with others, do arts and crafts to keep the mind and body occupied, and participate in travel activities to stay healthy.

For myself, I have yet to experience some of the serious problems that come with old age, because I have studied the Dharma and enjoyed reading books since I was a child. Because of these small efforts, I am still able to get along harmoniously with young people. It is good to really exert yourself in the area of reading, for that is one way to build wisdom and ensure that, as one grows older, people will still need you, for wisdom does not grow weary with age. It is also important to serve others and create karmic connections when you are young, so that when old age approaches your good reputation and good karmic connections ensure that others will be there to help you.

The elderly need the love, care, and spiritual support of their relatives. Family members should do more to keep the elderly company and talk with them; it is not enough to just make sure they get their three meals a day. In the past it was common for Chinese families to have three or even five generations in one household, but due to our changing society, smaller families gradually evolved. By contrast, Singapore is promoting the practice of the three generation household by encouraging children to live with their older parents, because when someone is old and sick, what they need and hope for most is the company of their relatives.

Modern parents work so hard to raise their children to adulthood, but once the children have grown up, they are like little birds that fly away from the nest. With the nest empty of little ones, the old birds naturally feel a loss. It is not enough to just provide for the basic needs of the elderly, for we must also enrich their spirit.

Today we have kindergartens and nursery schools. Perhaps in the future we need to establish "adult nurseries" to solve some of these problems. When people grow old, they enjoy chatting and sharing their past experiences, so it would be best if they could meet together somewhere and have some volunteers there to listen to what they have to say. This too is a kind of compassionate commitment. When I first began my Dharma teaching career, I had what I consider the excellent habit of listening to what older people had to say. All you need to do to hear old people's enthusiastic reminiscences is to nod your head a bit and give a few compliments. Just by listening you can become friends with many of the elderly in our society.

The problems of the elderly are concerns that most families will face. Even if there are no problems now, there will come a time when you will grow old. One should think about old age while still young, just as one learns to make preparations for a rainy day. One can learn a lot from the Social Security System which the United States originally put in place to guard against no one caring for you when you are old. Under the system, you pay taxes when you are young, so that when you age the country will take care of you. The whole world at present is actively addressing such issues as healthcare, social welfare, and support for the aged. Even within the private sector there are many charities and public welfare organizations that have joined the ranks of caring for the aged.

Fo Guang Shan is currently operating many senior centers, old folks' homes, senior care apartments, schools for seniors, and other such organizations. At these institutions, the elderly are guided in the practice of some simple exercises to promote their physical health, while chess, mahjong, and various kinds of art classes are arranged to help them enrich the later years of their life through such study and practice. The Fo Guang Shan Compassion Foundation has also established "fellowship service teams" who provide services to lonely and helpless seniors, like cleaning in and around the house, helping the elderly to bathe, washing their hair, and triming their nails, mending their clothes, and supplying them with other daily necessities. These teams also help the elderly practice their chanting and prayers.

In the past, it was very common for people in China to live by the expression, "raise children for your old age," but these days that is not enough. You cannot count on your children alone to help you in your old age; you should have your own savings. Additionally, it is important to care for your body as you grow older and to continue to exercise; walking is a great form of exercise, and I have long advocated taking ten thousand steps a day. It is important to keep an open mind as you grow older, so that one is able to look towards the future, even seeing beyond one's own old age, sickness, and death. This is a way to imbue one's life with hope.

How can we care for the aged? A typical way is for an old person to rely upon his children and grandchildren for support in retirement. A better way is for this old person to have his own savings to rely on into old age. It is even better for an old person to have developed good karmic connections, and be able to rely on these for support into retirement. It is better still for an old person to be able to rely on their wisdom and learning to support them during retirement. But the best way is for an old person to be able to rely on their faith to support them during retirement. By building up faith while one is young, when old age approaches one is able to read the Buddhist sutras, chant, meditate, and practice visualizations. With faith one is able to keep company with the Buddha, make use of the Dharma, and be in fellowship with the sangha. The friendships that one makes through one's faith are often the closest of bonds, so in old age one will not be alone or isolated. With faith, old people can live a happy, contented, and rich life. In summation, the elderly must be self-affirming and be their own masters. As long as they are able to do so there is still much to live for.

In each of life's phases, we must not be selfish. We must be able to open our hearts and think of others. Only a person who takes others to heart and who can appreciate and repay others' kindness, will not easily become disheartened at life's pressures. When we see that family members and friends are confused and unable to think things through, or when they appear aloof, we should take the initiative and help them rejoin the group. If we can find a way to regularly challenge ourselves, we can find the courage to accept life's difficulties. This way we are able to heal ourselves, grow, and mature.

IV

Race and Human Rights

I n today's free and democratic societies there are often loud cries about the supreme importance of human rights and the need to guarantee them. But this concept of "human rights" is something that only came into being during the last few centuries. Presently we are living in the age of human rights and democracy. Not only does everyone promote freedom, but they place importance upon civil rights and emphasize the unique dignity of human life. On December 10th, 1948, the General Assembly of the United Nations issued the *Universal Declaration of Human Rights*, the first article of which clearly states that "All humans are born free and equal in dignity and rights." The document then goes on to talk about the rights of citizenship, politics, and religion:

> Everyone has the right to life, liberty and the security of person ... All are equal before the law and are entitled without any discrimination to equal protection of the law ... Everyone has the right to freedom of thought, conscience and religion.

Other rights that the people should enjoy and be guaranteed include: the right to take part in government, the right of creative expression, the right to an education, the right to own property, freedom of thought and conscience, the right to freely participate in the cultural life, the right to privacy, freedom of movement and residence, and so on.

Generally speaking, the modern era of human rights can be divided into four ages.

First was the age of civil and political rights, which lasted from the sixteenth century to the nineteenth century. During this time the people rebelled against the oppression of the monarchs and demanded the rights of self-representation, freedom, equality, security, and property. Second was the age of economic and social rights, which lasted from the nineteenth century to the beginning of the twentieth century. The scope of the struggle was expanded to include the right to work, the right to social welfare, labor rights, the right to unionize, the right to health care, and the right to an education. Third was the age of minority rights, lasting from the turn of the twentieth century until after the end of World War II. This generation was characterized by an emphasis on ethnic and religious rights and self-determination.

The fourth age is the modern age of human rights, from the Second World War to the present day, and encompasses social rights, environmental rights, the right to protest, the right to privacy, freedom of information, and so on.

Human history can be seen as the history of the struggle to win human rights. In this modern age, countries around the world now acknowledge the importance of human rights, with some even promoting themselves as being founded upon the principles of human rights and guaranteeing them in their constitutions. But the question remains whether or not these rights will continue to be protected if they conflict with the ruling party or those who are in power. For example, the media is the voice of the people and should enjoy freedom of the press, but often times if they criticize the government or reveal its abuses they are shut down.

Whenever elections come around, some public officials will launch anti-crime or anti-pornography campaigns as a form of "spin control," or even engage in improper wiretapping. Political parties will engage in mudslinging, anonymous letter campaigns, and leak incriminating video footage as a way of winning votes by destroying the reputation of opposing candidates. Such actions truly make a mockery of what it means to be a democratic nation! Additionally, the meaning of human rights and each individual's ability to exercise them differs depending on their conditions. Those in high positions enjoy certain "privileges," the wealthy enjoy certain "concessions," and influential people have their "clout." Though strange, these phenomena are wide-spread and have appeared throughout the history of human rights development.

RACE AND ETHNICITY

The way I see it, an ethnic group should see itself like a family, yet from a lifetime of experience it seems to me that the closer people are related to one another, the more likely they are to discriminate against one another. When I first came to Taiwan in my twenties, the Taiwanese people saw me as an outsider. I was a Buddhist monastic, but many public figures in the Buddhist community did not like me either. On the contrary it was the members of non-Buddhist religions or members of the Buddhist laity who were friendlier to me. I was a male monastic, a *bhiksu*, but other bhiksus did not like me. Instead it was the female monastics, the *bhiksunis*, who were more kind to me. The closer you are to someone's in-group, the more likely they are to be critical of you. Even in a family with parents, brothers, and sisters, unless each member treats one another with tolerance there will be no harmony. Such a family would be quite unhappy.

Frequently, feelings of tension or hostility between different ethnic groups arise because of different ways of thinking or different customs. Thus the interests of these groups come into conflict. For example, in Taiwan ethnic consciousness is often manipulated by politicians as a way of inciting ethnic hostility. Such actions create divisions between locals and non-locals, and cause serious damage to Taiwanese society.

The United States is renowned as a haven for immigrants, and given the many immigrants from various races around the world it truly can be thought of as a racial melting pot. America is a country that values human rights; it cares about freedom and democracy, and opposes religious and racial discrimination. But even though America's many immigrants represent great ethnic diversity, the fact remains that there are still obvious differences in how each race is treated in America today. As long as no one touches upon these sensitive questions, everyone can seem to respect and tolerate one another very well. But as long as there is still discrimination, and different ethnic groups are not treated equally, it will be very difficult for everyone to live together in true peace.

In this world nations are set apart from other nations and regions are set apart from other regions, but it is setting people apart from other people that is the most dangerous. In China the complex relationship between the Han, Manchu, Mongol, Hui, and

Tibetan peoples has wrought havoc upon Chinese politics for over a thousand years without ever being entirely pacified. It was not until Dr. Sun Yat-sen's advocacy of "Five Races Under One Union" that reconciliation slowly began in these complex relationships among the races.

Racial discrimination can stem from geographic distinctions and differences in language, social custom, or skin color. Even among groups that share the same cultural and racial origins, there can be divisions in terms of relative wealth and position which form various complex orders of distinction that preclude the possibility of living together in harmony. Though intermarriage is becoming more and more common today, cases in which a white woman marries a black man are still few in number. It cannot be denied that there are still some races that feel as though they are innately superior, while other races are treated as inferior. What matters most is that each of us hold onto the principle that all living beings are equal. Only by respecting others within our heart can we follow the path to achieving peace.

INDIGENOUS CULTURAL RIGHTS

Culture is the product of human civilization, as well as its driving force. Each country around the world has its native peoples, and each of these indigenous peoples have their own unique culture which we should respect and protect.

Culture must not be infringed upon, but culture can be exchanged. All countries around the world today are absorbing the culture of other countries. Any country that wishes to refine itself must have a breadth of spirit, just as a great mountain accepts all of its different soils and the ocean receives the blended water from all of its tributaries without judgment. The more broadly a country embraces cultural diversity, the greater it will become.

Since I was a child I have especially enjoyed learning about China's own ethnic minorities, so much so that I once collected videos which featured these minorities and the way they lived. I have rarely had the opportunity to go to the more remote areas of China to visit these ethnic minorities, though I once made a trip to the Burmese border. There were sixteen distinct ethnic minorities who lived there, and I remember thinking that all the people there were quite beautiful.

Taiwan has its own aborigines, who were called the "mountain tribes" in the past. In recent years, the Buddha's Light International Association has taken the initiative and provided financial assistance to the aborigines, including constructing libraries and donating books. Such steps will offer them more educational opportunities, in hopes of helping them to develop the strength needed to compete fairly in society, while at the same time ensuring they can preserve the uniqueness of their own culture. This way the aboriginal culture can further develop and expand, enriching the world's culture with its multifaceted splendor.

Many nations around the world today are doing a good job of caring for their ethnic minorities who are now receiving the respect, courtesy, and special treatment they are due. No minority group should be ignored, because each and every one of them, no matter how large or small, possesses their own language and customs. We should see the beauty in these ethnic minorities, for the human world is like a hundred different flowers which are all blooming together.

Culture has no national boundaries, for culture arises through the natural development of a people. No force of arms can dictate what kind of culture should exist. Human beings can make enemies of other human beings, but they cannot turn one culture against another. Since culture is something that forms naturally, it must be allowed to develop naturally. We should not use our own culture to invade that of another. The ability to respect the cultural uniqueness of every region is the hallmark of civilization.

ON BEING A GLOBAL CITIZEN

Several years ago, I went to Brazil to chair a board of directors meeting for the Buddha's Light International Association. During that time, I was joined by a group of police officers sent by the chief inspector of Sao Paulo's state police. These officers cleared the way for me when I went out and also patrolled and guarded my residence twenty-four hours a day for the ten days I was there. Because of these connections, the chief inspector and I established a close friendship. Thus when my activities were concluded, he made a special trip along with his wife to see me at Zu Lai Temple, one of the Fo Guang Shan branch temples near Sao Paulo, in southern Brazil.

When we met he spoke in a deeply moving tone and said, "The Dharma is so wonderful, how come it has taken so long for Buddhism to come to Brazil?"

"The Brazilian people are very honest and kindhearted," I said, sharing my own sense of admiration from my trip, "They are well endowed with Buddha nature."

The chief inspector replied, "There are no native Brazilians. Anyone who lives here can be called 'Brazilian!'"

This was the first time I had heard such a thing, and I was momentarily dumbfounded.

The inspector saw I was surprised and quickly explained, "The entire population of Brazil is one hundred sixty million, the vast majority of which is made up of immigrants from abroad. Thus there aren't any real Brazilians. Any person from somewhere in the world who comes to Brazil can become Brazilian. It is because there are no native Brazilians that everyone is Brazilian."

I was moved by the inspector's wise words. I thought about how I had left Mainland China as a young man, and had lived in Taiwan for nearly sixty years now. When I again made a trip back to my hometown in 1989 after a long separation, the local villagers called me "that monk from Taiwan." At that time I had lived in Taiwan for forty years, yet the native Taiwanese still saw me as a foreigner and referred to me as "the monk from Mainland China." Even as I have traveled all over the world, no one has yet to acknowledge me as an American or an Australian. Later on, I prided myself on being a "global citizen." As long as the earth does not reject me, I can be a global citizen, and live by the maxim that we are all one.

When I travel to the various regions of the world to spread the Dharma, I see how the British, the French, and the Germans who have now established the European Common Market are saying that, "We are Europeans." The people of the United States and Canada are calling themselves Americans, while the people of Chile, Brazil, Peru, and Paraguay say they are South Americans. If this idea could be expanded, wouldn't that make all of us global citizens?

Every country in the world has its immigrants, and the United States has its own immigration policy. Put simply, when an immigrant first comes to the United States they can reside here as an immigrant resident, but after having lived here for a number of years they gain the opportunity to become a citizen. When I came to the United States many years ago I was surprised by what I heard. There were people who had immigrated to the United States who, due to cultural differences, would make derogatory comments about the country and say things like "Death to America." But if you're going to say "Death to America," why come here at all? Such people enjoy all the material resources and benefits of America, like expressways and medical care, and then they go around and say they do not like America. Later, after I had established the Buddha's Light International Association, its US members would participate in parades celebrating America's Independence Day, and I would always tell them to hold the US flag up high and say, "We are Americans."

If you have immigrated to a country, you should treat it as your home. I joined the monastic order at Qixia Temple near Nanjing, and there was a Buddha statue carved from rock on the mountain peak, lord of all it surveyed from up there. A visitor was curious about it and asked one of the monastics, "Which Buddha is that one?"

The monastic replied, "That's the 'flew-here Buddha.'"

The visitor then asked, "Since it flew here, why doesn't it fly away?"

"Well, having already come here, it made itself at home."

Some time ago, a group of young people wanted to join the monastic order at Fo Guang Shan, so I asked them, "Who does Fo Guang Shan belong to?"

The majority of them pointed at me and said, "Fo Guang Shan is yours; you are its founder and builder!" You can say that Fo Guang Shan is mine, but if you stay, can you not make yourself at home here? Thus the best answer is "It's mine." You should think,

"It is 'I' who wants to be accepted as a monastic resident here and this place then will be 'my' home." If you feel that this home is yours, then you will be able to love it. Whatever in this world is related to us will elicit a bit more concern and a bit more loving care. The Buddhist sutras often speak of how "living beings are the living beings of my mind, and the world is the world of my mind." The sutras even go so far as to say that "the mind encompasses the vastness of space," so that all of space is in the mind. What then is not your mind?

After the turn of the century there was a time when Taiwan promoted the idea of "desinicization," and the thought of it would keep me up at night. I was shocked; if I was "desinicized," then I would no longer have any ancestors, for they are Chinese. I would no longer be able to speak the Chinese language, nor would I be able to enjoy the Chinese lifestyle in how I dress, what I eat, how I sleep, or how I spend my leisure time. It was quite frightening for me, for after "desinicization," how would I live?

Taiwan should not become less Chinese, rather, it should become more international and global in its awareness. All people in the world are brothers, and it is by having this view that Taiwan can become great. This is what is meant when Buddhists say "A single grain of sand can contain the whole universe." Why should the mind be limited to a single country, like Taiwan? Not only can we embrace both China and America, but we can embrace the entire world, enabling each and every person to become internationally focused, cosmopolitan, and a global citizen. Only when everyone becomes part of one family can there be peace and happiness.

The people of the world should not limit themselves, or draw the boundaries of a self-made prison. Everybody should realize that we are all "global citizens." Because of the advancements in communication we already live in a "global village," where the distant shore is our neighborhood. Naturally, the people residing in this global village will be "global citizens." I hope that we can all carry with us the idea that we are all one, and that we can all coexist, and that we can commit ourselves to becoming global citizens.

INTERDEPENDENCE

According to Buddhism, we should not only see the family, the village, the community, and the country as our own, but even the entire planet and all of the universe can be seen as ours. Our eyes, nose, ears, tongue, and so forth each function differently, but they all belong to us, and we cherish them in the same way. Similarly, if your hand was covered in boils that were festering with puss you would not just chop off your hand in revulsion. You would wash it, apply medicine, and dress it, because it is *your* hand.

As long as we see things as "mine," we will take very good care of them. However, the world is not "mine" alone, for there are many other people who are different from us. But this is precisely why the world is such a colorful and multifaceted place. One can look at it like the Olympics: each of the national teams has their own dress, strengths, and style that is different from all the others, and this is what is so engaging about them.

People have different ways of thinking and different interests and beliefs, as well as being varied in terms of region, gender, and age. Yet everyone is vitally linked and interrelated. Nothing in the world is separate; everything is formed through causes and conditions. We should contemplate this causality, and see that human beings as well exist in dependence on many conditions, and that

other people are part of us. Thus, even if another person is not be-
having well, we must still be patient with them, cherish and praise
them, and provide them with a positive influence.

TOLERANCE AND COMPASSION

Tolerance is the effective way to advance the cause of peace.
Respect, tolerance, and living together peacefully—these are some
of the best and most beautiful values in the world. Within a family, the husband and wife should be patient, forgiving, and loving
towards each other. After all, it is the reason they got married in
the first place: because "I love you" and "you love me." For us to
gain the love of others, we must first love them. As Mencius said,
"He who loves others will be loved by them." We can only coexist
peacefully when we can love others like ourselves, and have tolerance both for ourselves and others.

If we wish to eliminate dissension among ethnic groups
and advance the cause of ethnic integration, we should emulate
Sadaparibhuta Bodhisattva* who said, "I dare not disparage you,
because you all will become Buddhas." Buddhism asserts that everyone fundamentally has the potential to awaken and become
a Buddha, thus Sadaparibhuta Bodhisattva treated all living beings like future Buddhas, regardless of how they might curse or
beat him. This is both a form of respect towards human beings
as well as an expression of compassion. Buddhism teaches us to
be compassionate, but even though we would like to treat others with compassion, we sometimes find it difficult to generate a
compassionate mind. What can we do to foster compassion? By

* *Sadaparibhuta*, in Sanskrit literally means "never disparaging." The
story of Sadaparibhuta Bodhisattva is detailed in chapter 20 of the *Lotus
Sutra*.

developing empathy and being able to place ourselves in the position of others and see their point of view, we can develop compassion much more easily.

It is not enough for the mighty and the poweful to simply refrain from oppressing disadvantaged minority groups, but they should follow the Buddhist dictum that, "Living beings who are sick require more loving care." We should show a little more consideration towards those who are sick, and in the same way, we should take more care of the poor and the weak. Only a country that can treat the weak and vulnerable with loving care can be considered great. In Mainland China there are regulations in place for all levels of the government to provide, in accordance with their financial capacity, the necessary funding to develop economic, cultural, educational, and technological projects for the national minorities. As for those actions that infringe upon their legal rights and interests, the minority peoples themselves have the right to petition or file a complaint with the relevant state organizations, and the relevant state organizations must resolve the matter in a timely fashion in accordance with the law.

Nations who serve and support one another should do so with the compassionate spirit of "the great helping the small, the strong protecting the weak, the haves helping the have-nots, and the wealthy aiding the poor." In the past, America provided assistance to Taiwan in the form of flour and soybeans, and now Taiwan too has established "agricultural teams" to go to such areas as the Middle East to provide assistance in developing agriculture. This is an example of a good international exchange.

THE BUDDHA'S VIEW OF EQUALITY

During the time of the Buddha, India had strict rules governing its social classes, dividing them into four castes: brahman, ksatriya, vaisya, and sudra. The first caste, the brahmans, were the religious class of ancient India. In order to preserve their own rights and privileges and to consolidate their lofty position within society, they used religious justification to divide Indian society into four classes with themselves at the top. Under this system, the other castes had to embrace and accept their authority unconditionally.

The second caste, ksatriya, was made up of kings and members of the aristocracy who were to be respected liked the brahmans. The third caste, vaisya, included most farmers, workers, and merchants, and was oppressed by the power and influence of the brahmans and ksatriyas. They were not even qualified to receive a general education. The fourth caste, sudra, was made up of subjugated peoples who were considered to have been born into this world for a life of servitude and slavery.

The caste system created an extreme form of racial prejudice. The gap between the highborn and the lowborn was very great; members of different castes could not intermarry, and did not enjoy the same rights and benefits. Sakyamuni Buddha, the founder of Buddhism, was born into this society with such disparities between the classes. He was a member of a royal family, and thus belonged to the ksatriya caste, though he never considered using the authority of his caste to exercise dominion over others and oppress the people. Instead, Sakyamuni Buddha called for equality and declared that, "When members of the four castes join the monastic order, they all become part of the Buddha's family, just as four rivers flow into the ocean and end up with the same salty taste." He thus launched a revolution against this system of racial prejudice and inequality.

The target of the Buddha's revolution was threefold: one was Indian society with its strict caste structure, the second was a theistic religion that lacked any ultimate truth, and the third was the selfish ego that transmigrates endlessly through the cycle of birth and death. Most revolutionaries flaunt their slogans about working on behalf of the people, but the people do not really gain any happiness because of them. Such revolutions are derived from a hatred of the enemy, so the means employed to carry them out are very cruel. The Buddha's revolution did not use violence, but was a bloodless revolution. His revolution was completely inspired by compassion, and used compassionate means to embrace and transform everything.

Most revolutions are led by those who started at the bottom of society and suffer their own lack of freedom, peace, and happiness, and thus are able to identify with others who feel this way, and join together with the masses to rise up and overthrow an unreasonable power. The Buddha's revolution saw him begin at the top of the social ladder. He was born into the exalted position of a royal prince and enjoyed a life of luxury; such people normally have no need to carry out a revolution. But the Buddha saw how many people were suffering oppression and so, for the sake of fairness and justice, he abandoned all the pomp and splendor of being a prince and championed the truth that all living beings are equal to defend the oppressed against tyranny.

Most revolutions are targeted outward, rather than being directed within. To put it plainly, they conduct their revolution against other people rather than against themselves. The Buddha realized that each person has a selfish ego, and is bound to the cycle of birth and death by their ignorance and afflictions. To be liberated and achieve true freedom, the Buddha understood that there was no choice but to direct the revolution at humanity's five desires of wealth, sex, fame, food, and sleep. In renouncing all of these desires, one is able to live a plain and simple life. This is the ultimate revolution.

Many people misunderstand and think that Buddhists try to escape from reality, and that they are passive and weary of the world. This is a great misunderstanding of the original intent for learning the Dharma. In becoming a renunciant and engaging in spiritual practice, the Buddha was seeking to deliver himself from the sufferings of life and death, though on the other hand he also endeavored to bring relief to the oppressed.

Sakyamuni Buddha abandoned his position as a prince to practice spiritual cultivation chiefly because of his dissatisfaction with the society of his day and its great disparities among the classes. This is why the first declaration he uttered after his awakening was, "All sentient beings have the Tathagata's wisdom and virtue," and he asserted that all living beings possess the same Buddha nature. Therefore, not only does Buddhism affirm an equality among human beings, but it also affirms an equality between humans and all living beings. The only distinction that exists in Buddhism is between those who come to realization first and those who do so later, what simply amounts to the difference between more advanced learners and novice learners. But in terms of their ability to learn and the dignity of their personhood, everyone is equal.

All life is collective in nature, and the formation of a particular ethnic group is the result of a gathering of people who share various factors including kinship, geography, language, writing systems, customs, habits, skin color, and religious beliefs. In contrast, owing to differences in innate or acquired conditions among the different races, equality cannot be achieved on the basis of external appearances alone, and so we must look to the original mind and inherent nature.

I have always kept the view that we should "allow for differences within what is the same, and seek consensus among differences." No matter what race you are or whether the color of your skin is white, black, brown, or yellow, everyone should be like brothers and sisters.

There will be many different ways of thinking among us, and we should allow for these differences, but among these differences we should know that we are all the same in that we are all human beings. We should focus on caring for one another and make the pursuit of harmony our shared goal.

Many nations contain immigrants from abroad, and many people are the children of multiethnic relationships. Brazil is an example of a multiethnic people. The indigenous people of early Brazil intermarried with the Portuguese, and later on African people added their bloodlines. Then came successive waves of Italians, Germans, Poles, Yugoslavians, Arabs, and Japanese who intermarried with the local people. Not only is Brazil a multiethnic country, but it is almost totally lacking any racial prejudice.

Seriously speaking however, the world's racial problems are not something that can be solved by politics, economics, or even religion. The best approach is the mutual respect and tolerance between human beings that recognizes the existence of difference. I am a Buddhist monastic, yet over the decades of my monastic life I have met Catholic priests and nuns, as well as Muslim religious leaders. I have treated them all with friendship and respect. There is certain priest named Father Ting Songyun who came to

Taiwan from the United States and once said to me, "If you had been born in America, you might have become a good American priest there."

I replied, "If you had been born in China, you might very well have become a good Chinese monk." We come to our different religious faiths owing to the different places where we are born, but our hearts are all the same.

There are many different peoples in the world. As individuals, we differ in terms of intelligence, body size and shape, and so on. But we can achieve equality within these many differences by being conscious of the fact that we are all one, and equal in human character and Buddha nature. Only by treating everyone equally, and with the dignity of the human character can we alleviate racial prejudice and reduce ethnic tensions. Then, and only then, will the world have its day of peace.

The classic Chinese history text, the *History of the States*, contains the following passage:

> A single sound is not harmonious; a single color makes no pattern, a single flavor does not satisfy the palate, and a single object leaves no impression.

We know perfectly well that other people will be different from us, but this does not matter. Just as clothes can be red, white, and yellow in color; or how tables and chairs can be square, rectangular, or round in shape, it is only through diversity in its many forms that the world can become a place of beauty and wonder.

How then can dissension among ethnic groups be eliminated so that ethnic integration can be advanced? What comes to mind for me is to remember that we are all equal in Buddha nature. Everyone should be respectful and tolerant of each other, coexisting together in oneness. This is extremely important.

In the ideal vision of the world according to Humanistic Buddhism, each person is seen as a global citizen, and together we all work for the good of humanity, without any racial distinctions. To create a Pure Land on earth that is illuminated by the Buddha's light, we must completely realize the truth that all living beings are equal, and ensure that there is no racial prejudice or class struggle.

Buddhism emphasizes compassion and tolerance, unlike some other religions that bring with them a strong sense of ethnic identity. Buddhism is basically a religion that preaches peace. The Dharma teaches people to treat friend and foe with equanimity, so that we not only forget the misdeeds of others and carry no hatred towards bad people, but that we even love our enemies.

The world was formed through the combination of many conditions, so it is not enough that we only love ourselves. We must love others so we can come together, grow, and persist. The greater the breadth of a person's mind, the more that person can accomplish, and the more that person can embrace within himself. If you have the capacity to love a family, you can be a parent. If you can love a city, you can be the mayor. If you can love the entire nation, you can be its president or prime minister.

In Buddhist literature, the phrases "the mind can encompass the vastness of space," and "make the mind like empty space," occur frequently. This is because empty space can embrace anything. If we can make our minds like empty space, the mind is then able to embrace all the phenomena of the universe. What then would be excluded? Each person should embrace the whole world with tolerance, and everyone should become a global citizen. Only when the world becomes as closely connected as a family will humanity have any happiness worth mentioning.

V

Politics

The Greek philosopher Aristotle said that "Man is by nature a political animal." The Chinese word for politics is made up of two characters, *zheng* (政) and *zhi* (治). Dr. Sun Yat-sen, the father of modern China, defined politics by saying. "*Zheng* refers to the affairs of the people, *zhi* refers to management; therefore politics (*zhengzhi*) is the management of the affairs of the people." More specifically, all the affairs of state as implemented through public administration can be called "politics."

The greatest function of politics is to guarantee the survival and security of the people and their families, as well as the society and nation as a whole. But apart from this goal, politics can differ wildly from benevolent to dictatorial policies, and from good to despotic governance. The way that those in power manage the government has an absolute bearing on the rise or fall of a nation and upon the security and happiness of the people.

National leaders who govern well implement benevolent policies. Through the love and value of their people, they will win support and enjoy a smooth and harmonious administration. On the contrary, those who act in a perverse manner, following ruthless and selfish policies will surely be despised by their people, paving the way for their ultimate downfall. Simply put, "Those who win the people succeed; those who lose the people fail."

History both past and present provides ample and persuasive evidence for this principle. In Chinese history, the *Records of the Grand Historian* tells of the tyranny of King Li during the ninth century, B.C.E., in the state of Zhou. The wanton slaughter of innocent people was commonplace. He created an atmosphere in which no one in the country dared to speak, but could only indicate their feelings in their eyes upon meeting each other in the road. Three years later the people rose up and drove him away.

Conversely, Emperor Taizong of the Tang dynasty was a wise ruler, and during his time on the throne, the nation flourished and prospered. The text, the *Essential Politics of the Zhenguan Era* records him saying to his ministers:

> In practicing the way of the ruler, one must first preserve the common people. If one does harm to the common people in order to benefit himself, it is like cutting flesh from your thigh to fill your stomach. Though the stomach is satiated, your body will die.

He also cautioned his courtiers by making an example of the previous ruler, Emperor Yang of the Sui dynasty, who was decadent, ruthless, and levied excessive taxes on the people such that they lived in misery while the empire fell apart.

Can one really say which country in the world is good and which is bad? Which nation is superior and which is inferior?

There is no universal standard for determining who is rich and who is poor, or who is honorable and who is lowly. In the past, the Chinese, Japanese, Mongol, and Indian peoples each had their golden age. Among these, the Chinese people in particular have always prided themselves for their "five thousand years of culture," and once considered themselves the most outstanding people in the world. But today they have fallen behind. The British Empire fought around the world and established many colonies in various countries, and came to be known as "the empire on which the sun never sets." But a comparison between Great Britain and the United States today would show just how far Great Britain has come down in the world. However, the United States cannot consider itself so rich and powerful either, for the world is impermanent. Take for example those desert countries of the Middle East which were once so impoverished. When oil was discovered beneath the desert, these countries became extremely wealthy overnight. How could we possibly look down upon them now?

Wealth, poverty, honor, and dishonor all change over time. The karma of all living beings seen in the different ways we think, speak, and act, will in turn bring so many varied effects.

THE STATESMAN

For an administration to become a place of prosperity, clean government, and stability it is important that a country have a few less politicians and a few more statesmen. In nineteenth century America, the Unitarian minister James Freeman Clarke said, "The difference between a politician and a statesman is: a politician thinks of the next election and a statesman of the next generation."

Surveying the political world past and present in its various forms, I would sum up the differences between a statesman and a politician as such: A politician puts his heart into being an official, while a statesman puts his heart into the task at hand. A politician thinks about benefiting himself, while a statesman thinks of benefiting others. A politician thinks of himself and neglects justice, while a statesman thinks of justice and neglects himself. A politician is shortsighted and is only concerned with making quick fixes, while a statesman is farsighted and thinks of long-term solutions. A politician uses his party affiliation to attack other parties, while a statesman can work with other political parties without losing his core values. A politician adjusts to his office with difficulty and is then unwilling to leave, while a statesman assumes the reigns of power with ease and is able to leave office gracefully. A politician has no conscience, while a statesman is imbued with moral courage. A politician schemes to get what he desires, while a statesman is willing to sacrifice himself for his ideals.

In my mind, George Washington is without a doubt one of the outstanding statesmen. He led America to its independence and then in 1789, he was unanimously elected its first constitutional president. He abhorred dictatorships, so besides doing his utmost to turn the loose confederation of colonies into a strong country, he also persevered in implementing a democratic government and thus laid the foundation for America's present freedoms and democracy. Washington was the kind of statesman who possessed a strong sense of responsibility towards the country and its people, and who had brilliant political foresight. Statesmen possess such noble character and such lofty political ideals, that even when failure ultimately strikes they still leave their illustrious names to history.

There have been times when those who would go on to be known as some of history's great statesmen used political tricks and maneuvering to obtain power, but having done so they then adopted a moderate approach, regained a sense of loyalty to the nation, and worked wholeheartedly on behalf of the people. One example is Emperor Taizong, mentioned earlier, who came to power by assassinating two of his brothers in what became known as the "Xuanwu Gate Incident." Such a step is no different from what many of history's ignoble politicians have done, but after becoming emperor, Emperor Taizong made great efforts to strengthen the country by seeking out earnest council and disciplining himself with strict standards. He called upon all talented individuals to join his administration, and in so doing established the world's most powerful empire at that time, creating "the great Zhenguan era," the only era free of corruption in all of China's history. Given his accomplishments and contributions, Emperor Taizong should indeed be considered a statesman whose flaws cannot obscure his merits.

Another such example would be Cao Cao of the Three Kingdoms period. He is known as such a duplicitous scoundrel that, in classical Chinese opera, he is portrayed with a painted face to show his treachery. However, he put an end to a long period of chaotic civil war and laid the foundation for unifying all of China. With his extraordinary military genius, he set up military farming communities in the north on a large scale and reorganized the civil service system. His efforts resulted in a clean government and a stable society, and so he too is an outstanding statesman and military strategist.

The path of a politician and that of a statesman are as different as night and day, though politicians excel at dissimulation and can often conceal their ambitions and sinister goals with artful speech and ingratiating manners. Being able to distinguish a politician from a statesman at first glance is not easy. We should observe their actions, not only listen to their words. Zeng Guofan, an eminent nineteenth century Chinese official and military general, once said to his family, "Only the sincerest people in the world are able to overcome the world's most fraudulent; and only the most guileless people in the world are able to overcome the world's most cunning." Over the vast course of history, a statesman will be commemorated for a thousand generations, while politicians will live in infamy for ten thousand years.

Politicians may appear powerful for a time, doing as they please, but they cannot last. When they leave office or pass away, their administration often crumbles away just as they do.

There are no absolutes in the world when it comes to who is powerful or outstanding. There is a saying in China, "Swimmers can still drown, boxers can still be beaten to death." Even a skilled boxer can still be beaten by others, for however strong you are, there is always someone stronger. On the other hand, those who do not know how to box will not become the targets of other boxers. Likewise, adept swimmers may end up drowning because they are willing to go into the water. But those who do not know how to swim will remain safe since they avoid the water. Sometimes smart people can be too smart for their own good, and a sense of superiority can turn into arrogance. Such things are hardly a blessing.

Politics is ephemeral, only morality and human character are eternal. Confucius said that the ideal government "Leads the people with virtue and maintains order with rules of propriety." Confucius believed that "governance means correct conduct," and said that when a leader's "personal conduct is correct, their administration is effective without issuing orders; but when their personal conduct is incorrect, none will follow orders even when issued." Thus, from political morality emerges political power.

GOOD GOVERNANCE

A good government is one that likes what the people like and hates what the people hate. Good government promotes the well-being of its people by reducing taxes, strengthening infrastructure, and developing a prosperous economy. Such a government would raise the level of education and culture, respect religion, integrate the races, and establish a harmonious, secure, and stable society. To provide a pure and healthy environment a good government plants forests, conserves water, and emphasizes environmental protection.

According to Buddhist tradition, if Prince Siddhartha had not become a renunciant but instead succeeded to the royal throne he would have become a wise and compassionate "wheel-turning monarch."* A wheel-turning monarch governs by freedom and democracy, and institutes a morally transformed politics that practices the five precepts and the ten wholesome actions.

The Buddha was born into a royal family and possessed a deep understanding of national politics. He states in the *Mahaparinirvana Sutra*, "Under heaven there are many ways. The way of a king is great, but the greatness of the Buddha's Way is unsurpassable." The Buddha's political and religious ideals were fully integrated and supported each other. He believed

---

* Such a king not only becomes a great and successful ruler, but also rules in accordance with the Dharma, and thus "turns the wheel of the Dharma."

that politics cannot reach its ideal state without adhering to the Dharma. In other words, an ideal government must add religious and moral standards to its legal system and politics before it can develop benevolent leadership.

The Buddha's teachings on the conduct of a benevolent king appear throughout the Buddhist sutras. In the *Mahasatya Sutra* the Buddha teaches that when the people have worries it is a danger to the country, and thus a leader should always think of the people, like being always mindful of the safety of a child.

In the *Teachings to King Prasenajit Sutra*, the Buddha tells kings to watch over and embrace all the living beings, servants, and great ministers within the country by applying the "four means of embracing:" giving, kind words, empathy, and altruism. In the *Long Discourses of the Buddha*, the Buddha says that "Rulers and ministers should be amiable and accommodating, while superiors and subordinates should respect one another ... achieving these two things brings long-term peace to the country."

In the *Bei Sutra*, the Buddha says:

> Being a ruler requires clear understanding: study the past and present, know when to be active and passive, temper force with mercy, be kind to one's subordinates, benefit the people, and give equally.

In the *Dharmapada with Parables*, the Buddha lists the five requirements of a benevolent king:

1. In governing the people, one should be just and fair, and avoid any unjust action.

2. Foster talent, and concentrate one's effort to provide education.
3. Diligently attend to government affairs, love the people, and widely cultivate positive merit and virtue.
4. Take no heed of malicious talk and accept honest admonition with discernment.
5. Purify the body, have love for oneself, and do not crave pleasure.

In the *Golden Light of the Ever-Victorious King Sutra*, the Buddha says:

> Regard everything equally, both the close and the distant. If one wishes to become a true Dharma king, then there should be no political factions within the country, and the name of such a Dharma king will be celebrated throughout the three realms.

Surveying social conditions at the time, the Buddha felt that the rise or fall of a country was related to the ruler's morality. He taught that when a ruler was able, good, and conducted a moral administration, then the country will prosper and the people will enjoy happiness. But if a ruler acted reprehensibly, then the country is doomed and the people will suffer. Thus the Buddha stipulated moral guidelines for rulers to follow:

- Live purely and without luxury, and fairly accept the admonitions of court ministers.
- Be willing to give, and share in the people's joys and sorrows.

- Ensure that the levying of taxes is done according to the law.
- Diligently attend to government affairs and have a love for the people.
- Maintain the decorum expected of a ruler.
- Ensure that the adjudication of court cases is done in accordance with the law and without any favoritism.
- Maintain amicable relations with court ministers, lacking any sense of competition between the ministers and the ruler.

The *Varsakara Sutra* in the *Middle Length Discourses of the Buddha* also records an interesting facet of the Buddha's views on politics. The sutra tells of King Ajatasatru's wish to attack the state of Vrji, who then sends his chief minister, Varsakara, on a special mission to consult the Buddha on military strategy. The Buddha knew the purpose of Varsakara's visit and, instead of answering him, he begins a conversation with Ananda, who was standing behind him, on the reasons that Vrji is strong and prosperous. The seven reasons the Buddha gave were:

1. They hold regular assemblies to discuss state affairs.
2. They maintain harmony between the ruler and his ministers, and respect between superiors and subordinates.
3. They uphold the law, know its prohibitions, and do not breach etiquette.
4. They are obedient to their parents and teachers.
5. They worship in their temples and pay homage to the spirits.
6. They do not violate the rights of women or girls.
7. They revere Buddhist monastics and respect those who uphold the precepts.

During the first and second centuries after the Buddha's final nirvana, India witnessed the rise of King Asoka, who conquered many small and weak countries through military force. Later on, King Asoka toured his conquered lands, and though both sides of the streets were lined with crowds of people welcoming him, he could see the people's hatred towards him in their eyes. King Asoka came to the realization that, though he had conquered their countries, he had not conquered their minds.

King Asoka later embraced Buddhism, and applied Buddhist compassion and kindness to help the weak. Many years later, King Asoka went on another tour, but this time the people of the entire country had been genuinely won over. They came out in droves to greet him with their old and young hand in hand. King Asoka thought, "Conquering their country through military force was not a real victory, for it is only by treating people with compassion and in accordance with the Dharma that their hearts can be won over. Therefore, the victory of the Dharma is the only real and true victory."

Asoka came to realize that ruling the country through military force can only make the people hold their tongues and that only the Dharma can transform the world and pacify the hearts of the common people. During his administration, King Asoka would send a group of his ministers on a tour throughout the entire country every five years to check on how the Dharma was being transmitted. He also set up many stone pillars along major thoroughfares inscribed with the Buddhist sutras. He believed that the more the Dharma was promoted, the more prosperous his country would become. Later Buddhist kings, like Kaniska, Siladitya, and Milinda, also followed the Buddha's teachings and employed the Dharma to rule their countries. They established a pure form of politics that went down as a moment of brilliance in Indian history.

The Buddha also advocated a council system within the monastic order which established the democratic rule of law to determine what was in the interests of all the people. The Buddha had brilliant forward-thinking, and one can see the roots of modern democracies in the meetings of the sangha twenty-five hundred years ago. A monastic assembly is held for ordination, the recitation of the monastic rules, and the confession of transgression, as well as various specific convocations and monastic business. Within a monastic assembly, some acts are handled as "single-announcement actions," in which ordinary or customary practices are proclaimed to the members of the monastic order. As no consent is required, the action is completed with a single recitation of the matters at hand, much like the routine work reports of modern meetings. In some instances a "double-announcement action" is made, where the announcement is given, and then repeated again so as to seek the consent of those attending. Just as in most meetings, all proposals must be discussed and agreed upon before they can take effect. A "quadruple-announcement action" begins with an announcement which is then read over three times, with the consent of the assembly being sought upon each reading. If those attending remain silent after the announcement and three readings, this indicates the lack of objections and the proposal passes unanimously.

In the monastic assembly system the opinions and the strength of the members can satisfactorily resolve all the various matters of the monastic order such that the monastic order can live a communal life harmoniously. One could say that this system is highly democratic in spirit.

In addition, the Buddha would often adopt an open and democratic style when teaching the Dharma. Sometimes he would pose rhetorical questions as a way of explaining principles to his disciples and other members of the audience. Sometimes he would respond to questions posed by a pivotal group of advanced practitioners for the purpose of clearing up any confusion in accordance with the spiritual capacity of the audience. Then there were also those listening to the teachings who experienced their own realizations and offered their understanding and ideas. The Buddha's teaching sessions were like scholarly seminars, in which lively exchanges of questions and answers enhanced the audience's wisdom and understanding. The Buddha excelled most of all at controlling the tone of the gathering and clearly perceiving the thoughts and capacities of those in attendance.

The compilation of the Buddhist canon after the Buddha's final nirvana was also conducted over a series of four assemblies in which a final determination was made with the joint efforts of all in attendance to examine and verify the texts. All of this demonstrates Buddhism's democratic attitude through its respect for the individual, its emphasis on collective creation, and its observance of the rule of law.

Today's democratic countries strive for what is open, just, and fair in all matters. So in continuing the Buddha's idea of respecting the wishes of the people, Fo Guang Shan has always emphasized democracy. At its meetings, anyone can present their views, and though there are some unavoidable instances of people going head-to-head on an issue, everybody uses their sense of self-restraint to maintain the attitude that the minority should acquiesce to the majority, while the majority should respect the minority. Once a resolution has been made, everyone joins hands in the spirit of cooperation and works together to fulfill the proposal discussed during the meeting.

RELIGION AND POLITICS

A king's influence may last for a period of time, but a monastic is like a Dharma king whose truth can influence ten thousand generations. Emperor Wen of the Sui dynasty once spoke in admiration of the Vinaya Master Lingzang:

> I am an ordinary sovereign of the mundane world, while you are the sovereign who seeks awakening and studies the Dharma. You use the Dharma to reform people into doing good, while I use the law code to prevent people from doing bad.

In my early Dharma teaching career I gave a talk called "The Buddhist View of Politics," in which I listed several points comparing Buddhism and politics. These differences are listed to the right.

There is the saying in Chinese: "A leader is like a boat, and people are like water. Water can carry a boat, but it can also sink it." Political participation is the right of a nation's citizenry, except for when one has committed a felony. Even members of the monastic order must faithfully fulfill their obligations to pay taxes and perform military service, and may even exercise the right to vote and recall. The government has the power to govern the country and the people have the power to influence the government. This is especially true today when human beings have so many freedoms, such as the freedom of residence, the freedom of worship, the

Politics	Buddhism
Rules the masses and maintains social order	Transforms the masses, purifying society and the minds of the people
Wishes that all can live in peace and security	Wishes that all can live with loving kindness, compassion, joy, and equanimity
Emphasizes the rule of law and discipline	Emphasizes self-discipline, compassion, and repentance
Preserves security and defends the nation	Provides relief to those who are suffering and supports the nation
Selects those who are able and adaptable to serve the people through power	Selects those who uphold the precepts and know causality to serve the people through virtue
Punishes misdeeds after they occur	Trains people to preeminently do what is right
Enacts provisional laws to suit the present situation	Speaks of universal truth which is timeless
Works indirectly through the law to bring about equality	Points directly to the mind, so that people may see their nature and become Buddhas
Looks for immediate solutions	Seeks long-term benefit
Sees world peace as a goal	Sees the establishment of a Pure Land on earth as a goal
Governs through economic power, military power, and authority	Supports the state with the powers of virtue, Dharma, and the mind
Begins with the external, and asks people to regulate their behavior	Begins with the internal, and asks people to regulate the mind

freedom of speech, the freedom of political participation, and so on. As Patrick Henry said during the American Revolution, "Give me liberty, or give me death."

Politics is an important part of social organization, for nothing in the world can remain detached from politics and no one can survive without it. Human beings are social animals and cannot live in isolation from the group. However, whenever politics is mentioned people label it as chicanery, manipulation, parasitism, and in-fighting. This is why Buddhists, with their emphasis on harmony, will often avoid talking about politics, and may even think that doing away with politics makes for the best of all possible worlds.

When the topic turns to religion and politics, most people feel that the two should be separate and not interfere with each other, that "what is religious belongs to religion and what is political belongs to politics." Though we can all acknowledge the importance of the separation of church and state, religion and politics can also complement each other and supply what the other needs. For example, Buddhism was able to influence the administrative principles of emperors and kings, and assisted these rulers in cultivating themselves, governing the country, and bringing peace to the world. Likewise, the propagation of Buddhism could only have expanded as it has by relying upon the protection of these rulers. Thus, political leaders and their ministers have maintained close ties with members of the monastic order for generations.

In China, Emperor Wen of the Southern Song dynasty appointed the monk Huilin as his prime minister. Venerable Huilin attended to the affairs of state each day dressed in his monastic robes, and was thus known by his contemporaries as the "black-robed prime minister." Emperor Taizong of the Tang dynasty asked Venerable Mingzhan to instruct him on how to bring stability and security to the country. Venerable Mingzhan advised him on how to use Buddhist compassion in his administration. The Yongle Emperor of the Ming dynasty was so fond of Chan Master Daoyan's outstanding abilities that he issued an imperial edict commanding Daoyan to resume secular life and assist the court in reforming governmental structure and discipline. In this way Daoyan contributed greatly to clean governance during the early Ming dynasty.

Venerable Xuanwan, who lived during the Sui and Tang dynasties, was invited by the imperial court to serve as a mentor to the heir apparent, and he instructed the heir apparent to practice compassion, reduce the killing of animals for food, and prescribed to him that he should especially not eat meat in the springtime and that he should observe the vegetarian fast days. Such a monastic is endowed with the detached magnanimity of someone beyond worldly concerns, and contributes their wisdom for the sake of the country's peace and the people's happiness.

Sometimes religion and politics can coexist in a complementary and harmonious way, but at other times we hear of religious groups that employ deviant teachings in a bid to overthrow the political establishment. Some such cases in China include the White Lotus Society, a heterodox "Buddhist" cult that led a rebellion at the turn of the nineteenth century, or the Taiping Rebellion in the mid-nineteenth century led by Hong Xiuquan in the name of "Christianity."

China has also seen instances of the governmental persecution of Buddhism, such as when Emperor Taizu of the Ming dynasty prohibited the laity from entering Buddhist temples as well as monastics from having any contact with lay life, forcing them to withdraw into the mountains. On other occasions there has been a clear understanding about how to accept Buddhist help. Today, for example, many governments will allow Buddhist groups to play a role in relief assistance whenever major natural disasters occur.

Buddhism influences politics throughout the Buddhist world. For example, the Thai king must undergo a short period of training in the monastic life before he can ascend the throne, to ensure that he has learned respectful monastic deportment and instilled himself with the compassionate spirit of Buddhism. Tibet has also always implemented the integration of religion and politics. For a time Buddhism was the state religion of Korea, and the Korean government sponsored the creation of a wood-block print of the entire Buddhist canon in hopes that the positive karma from such an act would protect the country. These examples demonstrate just how close the relationship between Buddhism and politics can be. Politics needs Buddhism's ability to transform people morally to create a harmonious and stable society, while Buddhism needs the protection and support of government for it to become a time-honored and long-standing institution.

Buddhism has long relied on political leaders to spread its teachings. As Venerable Daoan of the Jin dynasty said, "The Buddhist ministry is hard to establish without the support of the ruler." In the *Benevolent Kings Who Protect the Country Sutra*, the Buddha instructed the kings of various countries that they were responsible for protecting the Dharma, and that by doing so, "those below will emulate the actions of their superiors, just as grass bends in the wind." Evidence of this can be found during the Buddha's lifetime, for it was only because of the protection and support of the kings Bimbisara and Prasenajit that Buddhism was able to spread throughout India. As previously mentioned, after the Buddha's final nirvana King Asoka aided Buddhism's spread outside India by erecting stupas containing relics of the Buddha and sending Buddhist missionaries to teach the Dharma in places like Sri Lanka. Emperor Ming of the Eastern Han dynasty sent the Gentleman of the Court Cai Yin to India to bring back the eminent monks Kasyapa-matanga and Dharmaraksa to teach the Dharma, thus introducing Buddhism to China.

In Chinese Buddhism, the great undertaking of translating the sutras was accomplished in large part by the patronage of generations of Chinese rulers who established translation bureaus. Kumarajiva, the famed monastic translator, engaged in his translation work upon receiving support from Emperor Yao Xing of the Later Qin dynasty. During this time period Kumarajiva completed the translation of seventy-four sutras and treatises in 384 fascicles, including the *Lotus Sutra* and the *Treatise on the Middle Way.* During the reign of Emperor Taizong of the Tang dynasty, the celebrated translator Xuanzang translated seventy-five sutras and treatises in 1,335 fascicles, including the *Perfection of Great Wisdom Sutra* and the *Treatise on the Demonstration of Consciousness-Only,* enabling the light of the Dharma to shine throughout China.

Besides bringing harmony to politics, Buddhism's contributions to society also include helping with production, developing transportation, protecting the environment, facilitating travel, fostering cultural development, bringing stability to the army and people, establishing educational facilities, assisting in medical treatment and relief work, contributing to financial operations, and promoting science and literature. Buddhism's compassion can even help to transform remote areas, eliminate hostility, and reform the recalcitrant. In particular, Buddhism's five precepts have made a positive contribution to various countries' peace and stability, for as the *Gratitude Sutra* says:

> If ten people in a hundred family village were to practice the five precepts, then there would be ten simple and respectful people. If one hundred people were to practice the ten wholesome actions, there would be one hundred kind and reverent people. Spreading this form of moral education throughout the universe would produce millions of benevolent people. A person who does one good deed eliminates the possibility of one evil act, and being able to eliminate one evil act prevents a single punishment. One punishment prevented in one home means one hundred punishments prevented in the country. The king of such a country could simply sit on his throne and achieve peace with no government action.

Buddhism and politics complement one another. Politics leads the country and people towards prosperity and stability, while religion serves as its guide. One could describe this relationship in greater detail as such: To adapt to frequently changing personnel, political institutions exist as part of a specific power structure so that power is balanced. It is difficult to overcome the limitations of this power structure, and it is all too common that this causes a certain narrow-minded egoism, as each group becomes absorbed in their own part of the political system. If political leaders do not establish their policies on fundamentals like morality or the principles of cause and effect, it becomes very easy to manipulate them through political maneuvering. It is easy for such politicians to be controlled by the desire for power and the wish to have more, and this leads to constant conflict.

If the society has no concepts of karma or cause and effect, it also becomes difficult for the people to settle their minds. Law is only able to react to unwholesome actions after they have already occurred, whereas Buddhism is capable of eliminating such actions at their root before they occur. Thus Buddhism acts as a remedy for those areas where political power proves inadequate.

No one in society can entirely divorce themselves from politics. Although Buddhists try to not directly intervene, they are concerned about society and its politics. The typical Buddhist attitude is to be concerned with the nation's affairs, but to not interfere in its governance. Buddhism transcends politics, but that does not mean that Buddhists lose their enthusiasm for caring about society as a whole.

For example, Fo Guang Shan and its many branch temples around the world were established with the assistance of donors from all levels of society; they were not built with a single cent of governmental construction assistance. Politics involves the implementation and supervising of societal affairs. Being a person concerned with the nation's affairs permits one to serve as a legislator or to make recommendations, but not to serve as a police chief, mayor, or governor who directly participates in political administration. The current social conditions in Taiwan are chaotic, and the standard for what is right and wrong is in disarray, so I would not endorse the candidacy of monastics as national representatives in the Taiwanese government, but I would recommend devout members of the laity to stand for election. We always need people to concern themselves with reform and the affairs of the state.

However, this is not the case for Buddhism around the world. Dr. Ananda Guruge, the former dean of academic affairs for the University of the West, is a Sri Lankan who served as his country's ambassador to the United Nations. On one occasion I asked him, "What is the current relationship between Sri Lankan Buddhism and politics?"

Dr. Guruge said, "Sri Lanka has more than two hundred members of parliament, among whom nine are monastics—and excellent members of parliament I might add!"

I jokingly said, "Your Thervada Buddhism is more advanced than my Mahayana Buddhism, for it would be quite difficult in Taiwan to have nine monastics serving on the legislature."

Religion cannot separate itself from the county, nor separate itself from politics. Monastics need not hold office or manage political affairs, but they must concern themselves with society and its people. The rise or fall of the nation is the responsibility of every citizen. No matter what one's position in society is, no citizen can remain indifferent to his or her country.

Although monastics have left the lay life behind, that does not mean they have left their country behind or turned away from their homeland. Patriotism makes no distinction between "you" or "I," "us" and "them," or monastic and lay, nor does it require an important, high-paying position in government. I do not think there is anything wrong with patriotism; it is not having a sense of national identity that is the real problem. A country needs many Buddhists to join the ranks of those concerned about state affairs, so that they may employ the Buddhist teachings to purify the mind, reform the moral atmosphere, and preserve social order. Buddhism is expansive and shines over everything like the brightness of the sun, and moistens both the tall trees and the short grasses like a gentle rain.

As for peddlers, ditch-diggers, the poor, and the distressed, we can generate compassion in hopes that they will obtain the nourishing rain of the Dharma, so that they can gather together once more the energy to enjoy life. What more can political figures do? Buddhism will never abandon even a single individual. As mentioned before, if those in office have some religious faith and understand the nature of cause and effect and give and take, then they could exert a huge, positive influence upon the country and its people.

Over several decades now, I have come into contact with quite a few politicians. In May of 1996, former Vice President Al Gore visited Hsi Lai Temple, and during our discussions this good-natured statesman expressed his high level of support and solicitude for religion and immigration. He applauded the Buddhist greeting of joining palms, for he felt that this gesture represented cooperation, solidarity, mutual assistance, and tolerance. When I went to Malaysia to give teachings in May of 1998, I had a meeting with their Prime Minister Mahathir Mohamad. He identified with Buddhism's compassion and sense of equality. He felt that all people should harbor friendly feelings towards one another.

In August of 2001 Frank Hsieh, the then mayor of Kaohsiung and later Taiwanese prime minister, became acutely aware of the importance of spiritual purification because he had read the following sentence in the *Benevolent Kings Who Protect the Country Sutra*:

> Before a country erupts into turmoil, the spirits experience turmoil first. Since the spirits experience turmoil, so too do the people. When bandits arise, the common people will die.

So he led a group of top-level officials who came to Fo Guang Shan to conduct a "Tour for Purifying the Mind and Discussing Government." At the time, I proposed the following approach for them to consult in their political administration:

> Taking the many as the self can solve problems. Taking retreat as advance makes the world more spacious. With the breadth of mind that takes nothing as something, one can embrace much more. Taking emptiness as happiness can bring more freedom and ease.

James Song, the chairman of Taiwan's People First Party, once said that he had learned the "philosophy of being second" from me, for he wanted to emulate the monastics by being mindful of living beings. Former Taiwanese President Chen Shui-bian visited Fo Guang Shan on three occasions and said that he found encouragement in the maxims, "Where there's Dharma, there's a way" and "The political situation within the country must be stable," after the Taiwanese earthquake of September 21st, 1999 and the problems between Mainland China and Taiwan. He also advocated the practice of the "Three Benevolent Acts," doing good deeds, speaking good words, and keeping good thoughts. In 2001 I was invited to give a speech at the Presidential Office Building, where I proposed four suggestions to serve as the direction for future efforts:

1. For economic recovery, enterprises both large and small must coexist.
2. For a secure society, all the people must work together with one heart.

3. For ethnic integration, everybody must respect each other.
4. For the country's future, our vision must encompass the entire globe.

The generations of eminent monastics are not like emperors and ministers who take direct charge of the government, but their love of country is the same as most people. They purify people's hearts and reform social mores by employing the Buddhist teachings. They supply society with mental fortifications and spiritual armor and give comfort to all who need encouragement in times of trouble and lost hope.

Many people will invariably harbor incorrect views regarding the concern for politics on the part of Buddhist monastics and think that monastics cannot become involved or concern themselves with politics. In fact, since politics concern everyone and Buddhists care about society, why shouldn't they care about politics? Even the Buddha himself once said that he was "one among the group." Avalokitesvara Bodhisattva traveled to many lands by employing his thirty-two transformations, and among these were kings, ministers, and great generals. For the sake of living beings the bodhisattva used such political backgrounds to help build a Pure Land in this world.

Buddhists' participation in politics is based upon the love of home and country as well as compassion for all living beings, and is realized by embracing the sagely mind in an attempt to bring liberation to the world and its people. As long as Buddhists base themselves on the spirit of compassion and aim to liberate others from pain and suffering, their participation in the business of politics will lead to the expansion of tolerance and prosperity for all. This is incontrovertible.

POWER

The English historian John Dalberg-Acton made this famous observation, "Power tends to corrupt, and absolute power corrupts absolutely." Power tends to corrupt and there have been many people in the past and present around the world who have worked against others in its pursuit.

I once read an apt description of power: Imagine a person sitting in a chair. Suddenly, the chair changes shape and wraps its arms around the person, binding him down. Then the chair slowly sprouts roots and holds firmly to the ground. The chair will not let go of the person, such that the person dies and slowly decays, until only a skeleton is left. The skeleton remains in the chair, for even in death the person is unwilling to let go of the chair's armrests. Vast power has an allure that most find hard to resist.

It is sad indeed to spend one's whole life controlled by power, unable to be free. Fortunately, in a democracy the opportunity to "take office" comes hand in hand with "leaving office." This process of one generation replacing the last is the natural law of the world. For example, the old branches of a tree are pruned so that new ones can grow, and only then can the tree flourish. In the same way, if a country's political leaders or those in charge of civic organizations follow the practice of abdicating their position in favor of a successor, then there will be no divisiveness nor conflict, and the work will continue in a peaceful and successful manner.

However, most people end up striving for fame, power, and position by any means possible, and once they have achieved their goals they completely ignore the interests of society as a whole. They are unwilling to share their fame, position, and glory with the people, and may even cling to their office when they should resign, unwilling to let it go.

The various psychological desires such as the pursuits of love, power, influence, fame, and position show the harm caused by the three poisons of greed, hatred, and delusion. This is especially true for those who occupy a high position after seizing hold of immense power. However, nothing in this world can exist independently and all things in this world, including kingdoms, empires, and rulers, are impermanent. The famous Kun opera *The Peach-Blossom Fan* by the Qing dynasty dramatist Kong Shangren contains the following lines:

> I have seen the towers rise,
> I have seen the party guests,
> And I have seen the towers fall.

This is an excellent portrayal of what impermanence and the lack of an independent self mean. Understanding these universal truths keeps us from becoming bewitched by the vanity and sense of superiority that comes from a position of power. Otherwise, we get caught up in restless activity all day long, rack our brains to the point of exhaustion, and act unscrupulously, taking things by force. In the end, not only do such things lead to constantly worrying about success or failure, but they also create negative karma which generates unease in this life and suffering in the next.

There is a very appropriate story from the life of Madame Curie, the world famous discoverer of radium. One day a friend came to her house for a visit, and saw her little daughter playing with a gold medal awarded to her by the Royal Society of Great Britain. Astonished, the friend asked, "This is a gold medal from the Royal Society of Great Britain. It is an honor of the highest order. How can you let a child play with it?"

Madame Cure smiled and said, "I want my child to realize from an early age that accolades are like a child's toy, and are something that we play with only for awhile. We cannot hang on to such things forever, otherwise we will accomplish nothing."

Indeed, aren't honor, wealth, power, fame, and position nothing more than playthings? They can be taken up or put away at any time. One takes possession of power, fame, and position to benefit society as a whole, and they can be given up as well so that others may achieve success.

There are some people who are true idealists who act solely for the benefit of the nation and its people. Fame and wealth do not sway them, and they carry out their responsibilities in an earnest and careful manner. In worldly things, they accept what comes without forcing things, but they adhere tenaciously to the truth without letting go. Therefore, they are not ensnared by fame or wealth, nor are they shackled and constrained by positions of power. They are as free and unfettered as drifting clouds and flowing water, casting their fate to the winds.

The Buddhist sutras also teach that "trying to end debate through debating means the debate will never stop." This is like pouring gasoline on a fire: the flames will only burn more intensely. Ending debate with love is like extinguishing fire with water, and is much more useful. Buddhism teaches that we should strive to treat others with equality and without malice or partiality, while Christianity says that you should "love your enemies." If we were to try and think about these ideas in terms of mundane reality, we would find them hard to achieve or even to understand. Only by slowly aligning our minds with the Buddha and sages will we be able to appreciate the principles these teachings contain.

Good government is not necessarily omnipotent, but it must guide the people to what is right. From the sutras quoted earlier we can see that the Buddha's ideal politics is encompassed by the idea of the benevolent king, the wheel-turning monarch. He believed that a country cannot expand its military power to invade other countries, but that its administration must be workable to defend the freedoms, equality, security, and prosperity of the people. If today's political figures are able to commit to memory the Buddha's incisive views and ideas about how a government should be run and then implement them in managing the state and the affairs of the people, their actions would be a blessing for the country and its people.

What is commendable about democracy is that its people enjoy the rights of freedom and liberty. When liberalism began gathering steam, there were many people who praised freedom and said, "Life is truly precious and love is even more important, but I would give up both for the sake of freedom." However, with the passage of a few centuries, liberalism went from something fashionable to something excessive. People would shake their heads and sigh with regret, "Freedom, how many crimes have been committed in your name?" Freedom went from something that superseded life and love to an excuse for committing all manner of wrongful deeds, and become the object of people's denunciations. What was the problem?

In and of itself, freedom is a very fine thing. Yet freedom must not lead to harming others. On this point the various democratic countries have all drawn a clear distinction. For example, France's *Declaration of the Rights of Man and of the Citizen* states:

> Liberty consists of the freedom to do anything which injures no one else; hence the exercise of the natural rights of each man has no limits except those which assure to the other members of the society the enjoyment of the same rights.

Dr. Sun Yat-sen also stated in his *Principle of Democracy*:

> The infringement upon another's boundaries is not freedom. ... Freedom does not mean something sacred that cannot be infringed upon, and so boundaries must be set down in order to limit it.

We can see from these quotations that freedom and the rule of law are inseparable, for there can be no real freedom without the restraint of the rule of law. This is the only way that a truly democratic country can be established.

However, in the end the law is not the ultimate thing, for it cannot completely guarantee the life and property of the people, nor the right to exercise their freedoms. Only receiving and practicing the Buddha's teachings can thoroughly improve the human heart so that a state of peace and happiness can be achieved.

Buddhism and politics are bound together like our teeth and lips. History demonstrates that when Buddhism is more pervasive in a country, the country benefits. In the same way, Buddhism can only flourish when the country is prosperous and the government is fair and honest. Therefore, as citizens we should care about the important affairs of state, while as religious people we should do all we can to ensure happiness for all humanity. We must not remain indifferent, but be actively concerned and follow through with our responsibilities.

Human beings are political. We are concerned about society, and in doing so one cannot help but be interested in politics, for politics is the management of the masses. Human beings are social, and cannot be apart from the group. Thus the close relationships that are developed in human society are inevitable, as too are the politics that grow out of these relationships.

Buddhism cannot remain aloof from the concerns of society, the protection of human rights, and the welfare of the masses. It cannot hold to some sense of moral superiority by divorcing itself from politics. The Buddhist policy of having concern for a nation's affairs, but not interfering with its governance, means that an individual can be free of any craving for power and influence but not abandon the responsibility to care about society and serve the masses. To spread the Dharma for the benefit of living beings, not only should Buddhist followers eschew the passive attitude of avoidance, but they should be actively concerned and follow through with their responsibilities. This is the practice of the bodhisattva path in Humanistic Buddhism.

VI

War and Peace

Why is there war? Sometimes war breaks out between countries because one country violates another's interests, while sometimes there are economic reasons or contested territories. Even differences in religious beliefs can lead to war. Wars between ethnic groups can easily break out too, owing to differences in their culture or customs.

The fundamental reason war never ends is because of our natural tendency toward greed. There is a constant struggle to obtain more power, more money, more fame, and higher positions. In the thousands of years since the beginning of written history, how many wars have been fought between countries? How many wars have been fought between religions? Whether it is an economic war or an armed conflict, or if the war is fought over land, power, or position, in the end so many people will die and so much property will be lost. Even the energy of the earth itself is damaged. From all this, who is really the winner? There is a Buddhist verse that puts such lust for power into perspective:

Out of a mansion with a thousand rooms,
How many feet are occupied when one sleeps?
Out of wealth built up into the millions,
How much can one consume from day to day?

Once there was a great general who led his troops to attack a town and plunder the land. To boost morale, he told his troops that if they worked hard and conquered the enemy they would be richly rewarded. Each and every soldier was galvanized into action, and they stopped at nothing as they burned, killed, pillaged, looted, and destroyed. After the town was captured, the soldiers asked the general for their reward. The general then spoke to them with a generous tone, "I will give you a three-day leave to enjoy yourselves as much as possible. Everything in the town is yours."

The soldiers surveyed the scene before them: the townspeople were either dead or had run away. The soldiers wanted women, but there were none to be had. They wanted to drink wine, but there were no wineshops still standing. There was simply nothing left. At that moment they all realized that war is not only about death and loss for other people, but we lose ourselves as well. In the end, the love of war and battle brings destruction to both sides.

Such is the nature of humanity's martial tendencies. In the *Middle Length Discourses of the Buddha* it is said:

> With desire as the root cause, kings will dispute with one another ... nationalities will dispute with one another; countries will dispute with one another. Because of such conflict, they will come to hate one another, and they will take up various weapons to do harm to each other.

It is from greed, hatred, the love of fighting, and the willingness to take things by force that such violent action as war is produced.

The origin of greed, hatred, and rapaciousness is the ego, the "I." The formation of the Chinese character *wo* (我), meaning "I," is very interesting. The character looks like a banner set above the character for a halberd (戈), symbolizing violent struggle. Where does our affliction and suffering come from? They come from the "I." Because of the "I" there is selfishness, attachment, defilement, and discord. A single thought of "I" brings constant distress. No matter what kind of war occurs in the world, be it a good one, a bad one, a big one, or a small one, they all happen because of this "I." For example, being attached to my perspective, my way of thinking, my opinion, my ideology, my party affiliation, my country, and so on.

During the seventh and eighth centuries, the Arabian Empire was constantly at war while it expanded to the north, east, and west. The Crusades from the eleventh to the thirteenth centuries were military campaigns fought between the Christian and Muslim worlds in the name of religion, though in reality they were acts of greed and rapacity. These wars resulted in a series of battles in which countless numbers were killed or wounded. Take China as another example: Did each dynastic change not result in millions of casualties? There is no telling how many lives were sacrificed during wars both large and small for the sake of ideas, faith, and power. According to the research of historians in particular, only nine years during China's five thousand years of history were free of fighting. This gives credence to the verse:

> Heaven and earth, long-enduring,
> > will one day cease,
> Yet wars drag on and on
> > with no end in sight.

Buddhism advocates peace, but from another angle, Buddhism has its own struggle of a different sort. Rather than fighting with others, there is a battle with one's own afflictions. In order to subdue the demonic army of the eighty-four thousand afflictions and achieve the victory of liberation in freedom, we must wage war against our selfish desires.

I was born in 1927, which was right when the fighting between Chiang Kai-shek and Sun Chuanfang had entered its most intense phase. The next few years were also a period of constant warfare as the warlords fought for control. The year I turned ten, the Japanese invaded China, marking the beginning of the second Sino-Japanese War. I remember a time when I was a child, snowflakes were falling and I was carrying two bundles on my shoulders as we were engulfed in a wave of refugees fleeing the war. There is truly nothing more heartbreaking than seeing loved ones being separated. I fled from place to place following the flood of refugees. I grew up during the war and, at the age of twelve, joined the monastic order. During my early years as a novice there were times when I hid and slept among the dead, as well as having many of my own brushes with death. My life often hung by a thread.

When I learned where a battle was taking place, I would sneak over to see what the fighting was all about. I would hear the great "boom" of the explosions, and see the dirt fly as the shells hit. I saw people killed by gunfire, and even heard the sound of bullets whizzing past my own ears. On such occasions I would quickly find someplace to hide, wait a while, and come out again for a look. Sometimes I would chat with the Chinese soldiers, and sometimes I would play with the Japanese soldiers, who seemed to me at the time less inclined to hold grudges against children. I also remember one time when the American air force attacked Nanjing. The bombs exploded with such ferocity that they knocked us out of our beds and onto the ground. In short, I lived for eight years under a storm of shots and shells.

With the end of the Second World War and victory against the Japanese, the country erupted into the Chinese Civil War between the Nationalists (KMT) and the Communists (CCP). I remember how KMT troops would come to the Buddhist temple where I lived in the daytime, while CCP troops would haunt the place at night. At the time, I was attending classes in a very small classroom and whenever we heard a "boom" from outside, we knew that some people had just been killed. We would go out and take a look after class and find the innocent victims lying dead in the road. This happened all the time. During the Chinese Civil War, I was seized and imprisoned by both the KMT and CCP. Sometimes the CCP would seize us, saying that we were Nationalist spies and must be shot. I was only twenty years old at the time, and because I had joined the monastic order at the age of twelve, I had no idea what the Nationalist Party was. Other times the KMT would arrest us, saying that we were Communist spies and must be beheaded. One moment I was accused of being a Communist spy, the next moment I was a Nationalist spy. My life seemed to always teeter on the brink of death, and each day I did not know if I would live to see the next.

I came to Taiwan in 1949, when Taiwan was embroiled in the "Anti-Communist White Terror," and suspected communists were being jailed and killed. It was especially a problem for me as I was young and an easy target of people's misunderstandings. Venerable Cihang,* who was a student of Venerable Master Taixu and a man I admired greatly and corresponded with, suffered far more than I did and spent more than one hundred days in jail, while I was only imprisoned for twenty-three. Each time I was arrested I had no idea if I would come back or not. Hopefully describing these various incidents can give you some idea of just how miserable the war was in those days.

The Korean War broke out during the 1950s, and the intensity of the fighting was something truly horrific to behold. The Vietnam War happened during the 1960s, delivering heavy casualties to the American army. Now we come to today to the Iraq War that came after the American War in Afghanistan. Priding itself as the "world's policeman," America was actively expressing its commitment to eliminate terrorism and secure the peace, but over these many years it too has become bogged down in a war from which it cannot extricate itself. I remember the day the war started, as I was in hospital for an operation to have my gallbladder removed. At the time I felt that at least I had nothing to fear, because I no longer had any "gall." Although I was not afraid upon seeing battle

* Venerable Cihang was another early proponent of Humanistic Buddhism. When he passed away in 1954, his body remained intact and did not decay.

scenes, it was all so sad and terrible. To think that yet more lives would be sacrificed in war's hail of gunfire. Truly, what is the point of it all?

After the start of the Iraq War, some officials and economic experts in America and Europe were becoming deeply worried. They estimated that America's expenditures on the Iraq War would reach anywhere from ninety-nine billion to a high of 1.924 trillion US dollars, and that the negative impact on the world's economic development would be fivefold: skyrocketing oil prices, a sharp drop in the value of the US dollar, a world economic recession, tremendous costs for the war and post-war reconstruction, and the sparking of trade wars. Therefore, war is not the best way to deal with terrorists and violence, for the aftermath of war leads to continued hostility and warfare. We must change our approach by applying compassion and loving kindness, bringing relief and education, and building hospitals and schools to resolve their difficulties. Perhaps this would require more time, but it would make it easier to achieve lasting peace.

I can actually say that all of my eighty years have been spent in the midst of war. My sense of war is that it is something brutal, painful, and meaningless. How then are we to achieve peace, so that innocent people can be spared from harm? Life is precious, and being born into this world is difficult. In Buddhism we say that a human rebirth is as rare as a blind tortoise being able to poke its head through a wooden ring floating on a vast ocean. To sacrifice this life so senselessly is extremely lamentable. Given that so many people have been harmed this way, I wonder how those who start wars can remain so callous.

These are bewildering times for the world today: the strong exploit the weak, there is an unequal distribution of wealth, religions and races are in conflict with each other, and there are the disparities between men and women and among different regions. The reason these problems cannot be resolved peacefully has everything to do with our inability to live together with equality. It can be seen in the past isolation between East and West Germany or in today's disunity between North and South Korea and between Mainland China and Taiwan. Each side brandishes its weapons, keeping themselves in a constant state of tension.

But I do see hope in the impermanence of such actions. During World War II, Japan considered itself a great power, as did Germany. But in the end, didn't they both lose for being great powers? Japan did not become a great power because of war. In my mind, they must have come to the realization that they needed to become strong and resolved to do so because they lost the war. With a renewed effort to set things right, Japan was ultimately able to restore their country to prosperity once again. During the war, Japan used its powerful airplanes and bombs in a sneak attack on Pearl Harbor in Hawaii and destroyed America's warships and the lives of its people, but in the end Japan did not achieve victory, much less subdue America. Today, Japan does not need to employ warfare, for it can sell its electronics and automobiles to America. In this way, they have done more to conquer America than they ever accomplished with warfare.

By 1990, owing to West Germany's attitude of respect and tolerance towards East Germany, the Berlin wall was toppled and with it, the invisible wall within people's hearts also disintegrated. Henceforth, under the principle of equality and mutual respect the entire country could join hands to create a wonderful future together. If the peoples of the Korean Peninsula, the Taiwan straits, and the people of Israel and the Arab Middle East could rise to that level of mutual respect and selflessness, then how could peace not be far behind?

Living in this human world does not necessarily require strength to subdue others. The use of loving kindness and service can indeed instill trust in others. If every country can be more considerate of other countries and be more helpful, communicative, respectful, and tolerant to them, then I believe we could win true peace.

We must find ways to bring both sides together. A family with two brothers may become embroiled in dispute as they fight over the family's property, but if someone outside the family were to try and cheat them, the two brothers would join together to deal with that person. People living in a community typically do not see things eye to eye, but when the people from outside attack, everyone will pull together to resist such external aggression. So must we wait for an invasion by space aliens before we can join together and have peace in this world?

Buddhism speaks of "the dharma realms as one family," and as described within the *Flower Adornment Sutra*, all phenomena in the universe mutually interpenetrate one another. A single phenomenon becomes all phenomena and all phenomena arise in a single phenomenon. Everything exists in a state of mutual interdependence, perfectly integrated in an endless, unobstructed array of existence. When viewed in this way, aren't all living things vitally connected to one another? If we could view the world as a "global village" and realize that we are all one family, then when disaster strikes, be it external aggression, earthquakes, tsunamis, or typhoons, everyone would be there to care for and help each other.

THE EFFECTS OF WAR

War is not entirely a matter of slaughtering innocents. Some armies fight with values in their minds; some fight for the sake of punishing villains and thugs, some fight to save the people from misery, while others fight to defend their country. During war, it is also possible to express love and compassion, engender the aspiration for awakening, practice the bodhisattva path, and bring comfort to the injured. But of course, war should only be an instrument of last resort, so when war is not *absolutely* necessary, it is best to first employ other methods, such as the power of peace, morality, and inspiration. These are far superior to the weapons of war. One striking example can be seen during China's Three Kingdoms period. The military strategist Zhuge Liang knew that it would be easy to kill his nemesis, Meng Huo, but then countless more just like him would rise up in rebellion. Instead he employed the power of inspiration and the two later joined forces.

All wars are not equal, but how can the positives and negatives of war be ascertained? War kills and wounds countless numbers and destroys human history and culture, yet war can also facilitate human civilization. A country must be strong and prosperous, so it cannot completely dispense with a national defense and military weapons. Following the Second World War, the Pope called for world peace, and the Soviet Union's Joseph Stalin asked, "How many troops does the Pope have?" A country cannot do without military force to back it up, but neither can it completely rely upon such military force. For example, the United States has participated in the Korean and Vietnam wars; now it is embroiled in the Afghanistan and Iraq wars, and there remain many problems that have not been solved by these means. In addition to the fields of science and armaments, I think that such a big and powerful country like the United States should put more energy into such areas as civil rights, humane action, freedom, and compassion if they really want wars to cease.

As to which reasons for going to war are good or bad, there are many things in the world for which right or wrong cannot be easily stated. People often lack the correct conception of what is right or wrong. Thus it happens that for every question of what is good or bad, correct or incorrect, and right or wrong, there are points of view and advocates for each side.

Sometimes the causes for war stem from a powerful force invading the territory of a smaller country, sometimes it is due to racial prejudice, and sometimes it is caused by political calculations. If a war is fought with the idea that one side must wage war to put an end to war or force a reconciliation, then war too can be described as something compassionate and loving that subdues evil. On these occasions war is not merely about inflicting casualties, but can be an act of salvation.

No single judgment could possibly cover all cases. America's Civil War brought heavy casualties, but it did lead to the liberation of the black slaves and enable later generations of blacks to enjoy basic human rights. The United States dropped two atomic bombs on Japan in 1945, scarring the people of Hiroshima and Nagasaki in a way that could never be healed, and yet these events brought an early end to World War II.

That terrorist acts continue to occur one after another is truly the world's misfortune. The ruthless attacks of the terrorist must of course be condemned, and we must figure out a way to stop them. The most direct approach would be military retaliation in line with "an eye for an eye and a tooth for a tooth." However, as previously mentioned, "trying to end debate through debating means the debate will never stop." Retaliation is not the ultimate solution. Besides military retaliation, there should be other methods, such as using the force of public opinion, economic sanctions, travel restrictions, offering care and relief, as well as applying compassionate energy, and so on.

Buddhism both affirms and approves of defending truth and justice, saving the world, and dying for a just and honorable cause. However, in the real world there are times when these are invoked, while distortion, abuse, and misuse prevail. There is no last word on what is exactly good or bad, right or wrong, but we can be certain that there will be no mistakes when it comes to the positive and negative effects of karma. No matter what, all wars are cruel and barbaric. The tragedies wrought by the destruction of war, including the loss of home and country, the driving of people into homelessness, the wounded lost in exile, and the separation of family members, are truly too many to count. There can be no absolute victory in war, for there is always a painful price to pay, and this is a lesson which humanity must contemplate and acknowledge.

Buddhism and War

Can a Buddhist go to war or not? No one should mistakenly assume that Buddhism altogether lacks the courage and strength for moral integrity, or that Buddhism does not possess the spirit to uphold righteousness. However, in the modern world with the growth of science and the abundance of material resources, any issue can be negotiated at the conference table. There is no need to engage in combat on the battlefield with guns and bullets. When a fight breaks out within a family and its members curse and beat one another, it is already unpleasant, to say nothing of the matters of life and death on the battlefield. Such fighting is not worth it. I pray that every one of us can live peacefully with our family and friends, and slowly develop this positive way of living. This then can be expanded and broadened, so that one can live in peace with all the people in the world. Such an approach will naturally put an end to the scourge of war and then world peace would be within our grasp. It is my earnest hope that such a day will come.

Buddhism holds that there is not necessarily a military solution to every problem, nor can victory or defeat be decided upon the battlefield once and for all. We advocate developing compassion, eliminating attachment, broadening our tolerance, and understanding oneness and coexistence as ways to advance peace. Additionally, putting a benevolent government into power can be a substitute for war. Diligent administration and the love of the people can bring about economic growth, peace and abundance, freedom and democracy, respect and tolerance, cultural exchange, and so on. This is what victory truly means.

In times of war Buddhists have often played a role in defending the country and bringing peace. In the Tang dynasty during the An Lushan rebellion, Buddhist monastics supported the government's efforts to quell the uprising by selling ordination certificates to raise funds. Emperor Gaozong of the Southern Song dynasty invited Chan Master Fadao to come to court and give his council on state affairs. Through his efforts, Fadao was able to raise abundant contributions for the army and later went to the front with the troops to offer his stratagems. The Yuan dynasty emperor Kublai Khan was so moved by Chan Master Zhiwen's support and positive influence upon his rule, that he gave him the title "Grand

Chan Master Puan of the Buddha Land." The historical examples are simply too many to count.

Most people would wish that they could be greater than others, but once the thought of victory or defeat appears, it is not unlike gambling: there is always a winner and a loser, the loser feels bad, and for the winner to win someone has to get hurt. The *Dharmapada* says, "Victory engenders enmity, while defeat leads to self-contempt. Do away with the thought of victory and defeat and there will be peace without contention."

When winning and losing comes between ourselves and others then disputes pile up one upon another. But if we can genuinely respect others' greatness and be supportive, the oppressive atmosphere will naturally transform into one that is more positive and beneficial. Therefore, human beings need not declare victory over one another. Rather, we should try to convince others through our virtue. If you make your way in the world by competing for supremacy and trying to be number one, you will not necessarily be successful. But if you are able to live in the world and treat others with gentleness, you will obtain the respect and esteem of others.

When East and West Germany were unified, the people of West Germany had to undertake their share of the costs for East Germany's poverty and they paid quite a lot of money to cover the debt. This was something quite impressive. There is no such thing as innate enmity between human beings; it is man-made. As a positive example, I went to Europe recently and traveled among all its member countries. No visa was necessary, and when I handed my passport to the customs official, he would not even look at it. Later on, I had to actually ask him, "Please stamp my passport as a souvenir, so I can show that I have been to this country."

In the past under Chiang Kai-shek and Chiang Ching-kuo, Taiwan believed in "peaceful unification" with Mainland China. America too hoped that Taiwan would remain at peace and secure by maintaining the status quo. Indeed, not only should Taiwan and Mainland China be reunited, but the United Nations would like to see all the countries of the whole world become united and work together in solidarity. There is a saying in Chinese, "Brothers united for a common purpose are unstoppable." Humanity should work together towards unity, for in unity there is strength.

Reconciliation is necessary in the path towards peace. But in order for reconciliation to be possible both sides must have a generosity of spirit and extend a hand of genuine friendship, and they must have the courage to admit their mistakes and make amends with an open mind.

Whether the leaders, or even the members, of an organization or state can admit their faults is a key factor in their success or failure. Whenever China suffered from disasters in ancient times, the emperor would issue an edict acknowledging responsibility to put the people's minds at rest. In 1998, US President Bill Clinton shocked the country with his sex scandal. At first, Clinton did not admit any mistake and gave misleading testimony during court proceedings, sparking outrage in the general population which nearly led to his impeachment by Congress. He later courageously and openly apologized to the American people, and in the end won the support of public opinion and remained secure in his position as president. Having the courage to admit mistakes can secure forgiveness and understanding from everyone, and offer the person who admitted such mistakes the opportunity to stand up once more.

Today, Japan continues to not admit fault in invading China and committing the Nanjing massacre, going so far as to erase the occurrence from its history books. In response, China witnessed a surge in vehement anti-Japanese demonstrations. In contrast, after World War II Germany considered the Nazis to be a despotic capitalist regime and made a clear distinction between its past and its future. On January 27th, 2005, the heads of state from Germany and more than forty other countries around the world gathered in Poland to commemorate the 60th anniversary of the liberation of the Auschwitz concentration camp during World War II, and to conduct a series of soul-searching events about the war.

From the actions of Germany and Japan, we can see how the forgiveness of others cannot be won without the courage to admit mistakes, nor can we achieve security and tranquility without forgiving others. People are not afraid of making mistakes, but they do fear lacking the courage to admit these mistakes. This type of courage is a fine virtue that must be present between parents and children, teachers and students, and among friends. Even between superiors and subordinates there can be a gentle harmony that provides space for each side to grow.

What goes on between nations involves a much wider spectrum, since a single policy, a single command, or a single action can impact the lives and fortunes of people in the tens, if not hundreds of millions. How can there not be caution? How could it be possible not to change when mistakes have been made, to ensure that such mistakes are not repeated again and again?

How can we free ourselves from hatred? The *Eight Realizations of a Bodhisattva Sutra* tells us that a bodhisattva "does not recollect past unwholesome deeds committed against him." We should tolerate others with great magnanimity, just as the depths of the great ocean can receive any filth and still remain pure, or the vastness of the sky is able to encompass all things, beautiful or ugly, and still remain boundless. The *Sutra of Illuminating Light* says:

> Do not return hatred with hatred, for in the end hatred will never cease. The practice of patience will bring an end to hatred. This is the Buddha's teaching.

Only repaying hatred with virtue can curtail the tangled web of enmity and resentment. For example, during the time of the Buddha, the Buddha's wicked cousin Devadatta repeatedly opposed the Buddha, and even tried to kill him on several occasions. However, chapter 40 of the *Four-Part Vinaya* tells us that when Devadatta fell ill and none of the doctors could do anything for him, it was the Buddha who cared enough to visit him and heal his illness.

The *Sutra on Upasaka Precepts* says, "The receiving of a small kindness should be greatly rewarded; any hatred directed at you should always be treated with kindness." With an understanding of karma we should treat everything around us with kindness. In this way you can become more empathetic and thus extinguish the fires of anger and hatred. In the end, unreconciled hatred will never end. Even though we should not erase the past, blindly seeking revenge will only deepen hatred. All we can do is learn these lessons proactively and try to put an end to our unwholesome tendencies, so that fundamental progress can be made in mutual understanding and cooperation. This is the only way to live in peace over the long term. The *Sutra of Teachings Bequeathed by the Buddha* states:

> Those who are able to practice patience can indeed be known as great and powerful ones. Those who cannot happily endure the poison of calumny, ridicule, or harsh insult like the drinking of sweet dew, cannot be called wise ones who have entered the Way.

Generally speaking, it is easier to put up with poverty, hunger, sickness, hardship, and tiredness than it is to deal with the agony of humiliation, injustice, and animosity.

Patience is not an act of cowardice. True practitioners of the bodhisattva path are able to patiently endure hatred, verbal abuse, and merciless beatings without retaliating in any way. Their hearts remain unmoved by gain, loss, esteem, slander, praise, criticism, pleasure, or pain. No affliction is able to sully them. They take patience and compassion as their strength, and can do what is difficult to do and bear what is difficult to bear. This is how they are able to eliminate the myriad forms of trouble and benefit all living beings. Therefore, patience is actually the most revered power of tolerance in the world, as well as the greatest force for peace in the universe!

Buddhism reminds us that the most terrible enemy in the world does not exist outside; our enemy is an army of eighty-four thousand afflictions including greed, hatred, and delusion that exists within our own mind. The *Sutra in Forty-two Sections* says:

> When a person takes up the spiritual path, it is like one man going to battle ten thousand. Clad in armor with spear in hand, the warrior goes out to fight. Those who are irresolute and cowardly will

retreat right away, or will turn around halfway along. Some will do battle and die in the process, while others will win a great victory and return to their native land to be honored with high position.

This section describes monastic practice as a war against our afflictions. Those who are timid and weak by nature will give up halfway. Only those with determination and commitment are able to achieve final victory. The opponent represents our afflictions, such as ignorance, greed, jealously, hatred, and laziness—all far more terrible than real enemies. They can disturb us such that we find it impossible to live a quiet and peaceful life. How can we subdue the demonic army of the mind?

Use Introspection to Scout
In Buddhism there is a saying, "Do not fear when thoughts arise, just fear that you reflect upon them too late." Zengzi, a prominent disciple of Confucius, was also known to reflect upon himself three times each day. Those who are able to engage in self-reflection and examination will not easily make mistakes, but when they do they can correct themselves immediately.

Use a Sense of Shame to Self-Reflect
The *Sutra of Teachings Bequeathed by the Buddha* says, "Being clothed with a sense of shame is first among all the adornments." People are not sages. Who can say they are without fault? As long as we feel a sense of shame and sincerely repent when we do something wrong, we will keep our spirit pure.

Make Right View Your Armor

On the battlefield, armor can withstand the powerful blows of the enemy and protect our bodies. Right view can serve as mental armor by resisting external temptations. What is called "right view" in Buddhism means understanding karma and the positive and negative effects of karma, as well as the universal truth of impermanence, suffering, and emptiness. Such a view is able to repel wrong thoughts, and helps us to turn away from afflictions.

Make Wisdom Your Sword

Manjusri Bodhisattva, the bodhisattva of wisdom, is commonly depicted holding a sword to symbolize how wisdom can cut down the army of afflictions. The *Sutra on the Mahayana Practice of the Six Perfections* says, "By employing the sword of wisdom, one can cut down the bandits of affliction, crush the army of birth and death, subdue the demonic force of Mara,* and bear every burden. In this way one brings liberation to all sentient beings."

Make Diligence Your Strength

In all things one must have the diligence and courage needed for going into battle. It is only by remaining free of fear or cowardice that the opposing ranks can be broken and difficulties overcome.

Make Compassion Your Strategy

Hatred causes people to lose their reason, such that they will stop at nothing to destroy all in their path. Hatred cannot bring an end to hatred. Only compassion can dissolve hatred, and eliminate the discord between ourselves and others.

---

* *Mara* refers both to a malevolent celestial being who opposes Buddhism, as well as negative mental qualities that cause practitioners to stray from the path.

Make the Six Perfections Your Army
By commanding the great army of the six perfections—giving, morality, patience, diligence, meditative concentration, and prajna-wisdom—one can vanquish affliction, reach the shore of nirvana, and leave behind the delusion of the cycle of birth and death.

Make the True Mind Your Commander
The six sense organs of the eyes, ears, nose, tongue, body, and mind are like thieves that steal our merit and virtue and lead us down the road of negative karma. But they are only able to perpetrate this act because there is no wise leader in charge. If we can recover our intrinsic Buddha nature and put it in charge, then we can walk down the path that is broad and bright.

THE PATH TO PEACE

Every person living on this planet hungers for peace. We wish to live a life of stability and happiness without war and fear. But as long as there is discord in the mind, and discord in the conditions of the external world, we will never experience a day of peace. Placing emphasis on such external measures as limiting military action or banning nuclear weapons while ignoring the purification of the mind will not lead to a true and lasting peace.

The root cause behind the world's unending warfare is our ignorant attachment to the self and our desire for power and fame. Therefore, we must begin with purifying the spirit if we want to remove the root cause of chaos in the world. To realize peace in the human mind we must delve into the mind. Putting into practice the Buddhist ideals of selflessness, compassion, respect, and equality can help us to achieve real peace.

We can use the contemplation of non-self to strive for peace. The "I" is the source of discord. The "Parables" chapter of the *Lotus Sutra* says, "A deepening of the sense of self increases hatred." Non-self leads to impartiality, impartiality leads to unselfishness, and unselfishness leads to peace. The Buddha once instructed the monastic order:

> If your clothes are torn through carelessness, the mind will experience despair, but if a leaf lands beside you, the mind will take no offense whatsoever. This is so because your clothing will generate the defilement of desire through the attachment to self, while the leaf is unrelated to you and does not generate the defilement of desire.

When teaching the Dharma, the Buddha would often explain the teaching of non-self by showing how what we think of as the self arises through causes and conditions. He would try to correct people's mistaken view that the self has a core or essence. By understanding non-self and benefiting others we become free of dissension and bias. If we want peace, and wish to follow the path of purity, we must eliminate the mind's attachment to the self.

Loving kindness and compassion puts peace into practice. Loving kindness and compassion are the foundation of the Dharma. There is a saying in Buddhism that sums this up quite nicely:

> All teachings that lack loving kindness and
> compassion are the corrupt Dharma,
> All teachings that embody loving kindness and
> compassion are the Buddha's Dharma.

Buddhist loving kindness and compassion are unconditional and see all living beings as one, which allows it to bring relief and deliverance to all who suffer hardships or distress. Loving kindness and compassion do not only mean to avoid harm, but specifically to do what is good. This is not a fleeting slogan, but requires considerable dedication and effort. We should not act with loving kindness and compassion solely for the hope of some future reward, but do so without expecting compensation. If we have this attitude, then when we see another person in pain, we can use our compassion to alleviate their suffering. The *Mahaparinirvana Sutra* says, "Loving kindness brings an end to greed, compassion brings an end to hatred." If everyone treated each other with loving kindness and compassion, then all living beings could be happy.

Another way to seek peace is through being respectful. We all enjoy being respected by others, but we can easily forget to be respectful ourselves. Fundamental to respect is the Confucian dictum, "Do not do unto others what you would not wish done unto you." When there is a lack of respect then jealousy, suspicion, and contempt arise. How then can people live together in peace? When there is no respect, peace cannot last. Any hope for a lasting peace requires the establishment of respect.

A mutual disrespect between military leadership and civil leadership is common. However, during China's Warring States Period, the mutual respect between Senior Minister Lin Xiangru and General Lian Po in the state of Zhao allowed the civil and military leadership to work together in peace. Because of this cooperation, the state of Zhao was spared from the aggressions of their powerful neighbors.

To actively work towards peace, it is important that we work towards equality, for equality and peace are two sides of the same coin. Upon the Buddha's enlightenment the first thing he uttered was, "Marvelous, marvelous! All sentient beings have the Tathagata's wisdom and virtue." This declaration of equality between living beings and the Buddha has since been a beacon of light which has liberated trillions of beings.

The Buddha himself was a model of equality. He put in place the "six points of reverent harmony" to promote the harmony in the sangha through maintaining kind words, thoughts, and deeds and holding similar moral standards and viewpoints. The Buddha would frequently say that "The monastic order is not mine to possess, for I too am one among the group." The Buddha would also often wash the body of sick monastics and mend the robes of blind disciples. The Buddha affirmed equality in so many of his policies, emphasizing that all beings possessed Buddha nature, that monasticism was open to both men and women as well as all the castes of ancient India, and that beginners should not be underestimated. The Buddha lived with the members of the monastic community with a sense of equality, never acting as lord and master. By the Buddha's example we can appreciate Buddhism's style of harmony, practicality, and equality.

Equality demands mutual respect, and that means not using coercive measures to force others into submission. Equality also demands the ability to understand another person's point of view and show consideration for the other side. This is the only way to coexist. The pursuit of world peace demands the establishment of equality, which means that all races and nations big and small must be able to coexist. World peace is not possible unless equality is present.

Peace and freedom are the highest pursuits of the spiritual life, and they are even more pertinent in this modern age where right and wrong are turned upside down and wars are frequent. We hunger for peace. But, if we wish to attain world peace, we must accomplish six things:

1. Spread compassion amidst hatred.
2. Offer forgiveness in place of hostility.
3. Foster faith in times of doubt.
4. Bring the light of wisdom to the darkness of ignorance.
5. Raise the spirit of hope and optimism in times of frustration and hardship.
6. Give comfort in times of sadness.

If everyone can commit to becoming an "emissary for peace," and put these six points into practice, then I believe that the days of lasting peace in the world will soon arrive.

The Future of Peace

As the Second World War was coming to a close, President Roosevelt sent a telegram to China, asking Venerable Taixu, a Chinese Buddhist reformer and pioneer of modern Humanistic Buddhism, the following question: "What plan does Buddhism have for world peace?"

Taixu replied, "Non-self, loving kindness, and compassion can achieve peace."

Can non-self, loving kindness, and compassion really lead to world peace? Non-self does not mean that "I" am dead or that there is no self. Rather, non-self means being able to break down and eliminate the attachments to "my ideas," "my opinions," "my beliefs," and "what I want to do." Since this world belongs to no single person but is held in common by all, we must respect and tolerate the differing ideas, opinions, and aspirations of others. Loving kindness and compassion means treating others well, and it is easier to be kind and compassionate when one is able to adopt the other's point of view. Non-self and compassion are far from trivial, and their expansion and development can indeed lead to world peace.

No one should lose faith in peace. Did the Berlin Wall, the very epitome of stony hostility, not come down? War and peace are both manmade. If our hearts remain full of hatred, and we spend our time thinking about how to use force to subdue others, then of course world peace is impossible. What matters most is that each one of us hold on to the principle of equality for all living beings. Only if we hold this in our hearts, will we open the path to achieving peace.

We all live here on this planet together, and we are all intimately related. Wherever two or more people exist, there will be war; with contact and conflict there will be harm. But all life is interconnected, and humanity can only attain peace through solidarity and friendship. "Solidarity" here means joining in solidarity with others, not that others must come and join us. Peace means that we are at peace with others, not that we expect others to bring peace to us. Anything that requires others to do something first will be harder to achieve. Peace begins when each of us takes the initiative to have goodwill. Positive effects will only arise from positive causes, that is the law of karma. Every country should try to be trustworthy, virtuous, and act with loving kindness, compassion, joy, and equanimity. Each state should strive to be tolerant of what differs from themselves, refrain from invading and subjugating others, and deal with others in the spirit of non-self.

If we can accomplish this, how can anyone say that world peace is not possible?

VII

Happiness

L ife has many tastes, as it includes both the sorrow of part-
ing and the joy of reunion. Certainly everyone wishes to be
happy, but what is happiness? Some moments of happiness are
familiar to us: doing well on an examination, being successful in
our careers, having a happy family, being financially secure, the
birth of a child, and the overcoming of hardships are all different
levels of happiness.

The happiness of life can be divided into two major catego-
ries: external happiness and internal happiness. External happiness comes from our senses, and includes pleasant sights, sounds,
smells, tastes, and feelings. Internal happiness is a more spiritual
type of satisfaction. For those who enjoy reading, nothing beats
traveling through the imaginary time machine of the printed word.
For those who like to write, creative writing brings them great
delight. For those who meditate, nothing can compare to the peace
of mind that comes from sitting with one's eyes closed as a stick of
incense burns slowly down. For religious people, there is no better
place than within their religious faith.

But if there is so much happiness in life, why do Buddhist teachers talk so much about life's troubles? Not only do we talk about all manner of physical and mental suffering, but there is constant talk of the impermanence of life. Even the very wealthy who have never known what it is like to go without food or shelter can have everything taken away by the next natural disaster, man-made calamity, or through the avarice or foolishness of some wayward child.

While it is true that no person has not experienced the suffering of impermanence, we all tend to forget our pain when we are surrounded by pleasure. There are many people who start out their careers hardworking and frugal, but once they have become rich and successful the lessons they learned from their life of hardship are pushed to the back of the their minds, and they start to spend money without restraint. Those who suffer from painful diseases will search high and low to receive the proper treatment and follow the right regimen to regain their health. But once these people recover, so many of them resume their old lifestyle of excessive eating and irregular sleep.

The reason Buddhists talk so much about suffering is to encourage us to accept it as a challenge, to endure it, take it as a touchstone in life, and to triumph. We should face suffering, find its source, and come up with a solution to remove it if we want to regain a complete and happy life. Buddhists are not misanthropists or nihilists. Buddhists talk about suffering in order to transcend it.

Life is a tapestry woven together with suffering and happiness. Since all things are impermanent, we need not fear suffering, for it will not last. As long as we face reality and weather our difficulties, in the end the hard-earned fruits of happiness await us. On the other hand, happiness is not to be reveled in, for if we revel in happiness without moving forward, it will fade to impermanence as well, and sadness awaits on the other side.

It is the nature of all living beings to pursue joy and avoid suffering. Worldly happiness, whether internal or external, is not the ultimate, long-lasting, true form of happiness.

There has been a story circulating on the internet that I have found very meaningful. Once there was a housewife who was tidying up after the rest of the family had left the home. After she had finished her chores she went outside to take out the garbage, and saw four men trembling in the wind. The men looked cold and hungry, and she felt sorry for them, so she kindly said, "Would the four of you like to come in for a cup of tea to warm you up?"

The four men looked at the housewife, and one asked, "Is anyone else at home right now?"

"My husband and children are either at work or at school, so no one else is home."

One of the old men said, "Thank you, but it would not be proper for us to enter."

The housewife returned home. Soon her husband and children returned for lunch, and she related to them what had happened. Moved by his wife's compassion, her husband said, "Go outside and take a look again. If the old men are still there, why don't you invite them in for lunch?"

The housewife went and looked and the four men were right where they had been earlier. The housewife told the old men, "My husband and children are home now, and we would like to invite you for lunch. Please come inside."

One of the four men stood up, "There are four of us here," he said as he motioned towards each member of the group, "One of us is named Wealth, one is named Success, one is named Well-being, and my name is Love. Only one of us will enter your home as a representative, so who would you like to invite in?"

Surprised, the housewife thought it best to return home and ask her husband. After he learned of the strange circumstances he said, "Wealth is best, let's invite wealth to come in."

But the housewife disagreed, "Why don't we invite Well-being to come in?"

Their son decided to add his opinion, "What about Success? We should invite Success!"

Their young daughter finally piped up and said, "Love is best. It would be much better if we invited love."

After hearing the words of their little girl, the family came to an agreement, and the housewife left the home to invite Love for lunch. The housewife encountered the four old men right where they had been before and told them, "If only one of you would like to come in as a representative, we would like to invite Love to come to our home."

The old man named Love stood up and began to follow the housewife home, with the three other men soon following him. Puzzled, the housewife asked, "I thought you said only one of you would come in? Why is it that all of you are coming together?"

One of the other men replied, "The three of us have this habit: wherever Love goes, we follow as well."

The *Treasure Box Sutra* says:

> Those who love their own life will not take life. Those who love their wealth will not steal. Those who love their own wives will not commit adultery.

Everyone wishes to be wealthy, successful, and to have well-being, but love is more important than all of these. The love that most people have is a conditioned form of love. Owing to all the differences in proximity and interest there are compromises and calculations which lead to discord between ourselves and other people. When the whole family, the husband, wife, father, mother, sons, daughters, relatives, and friends, can love one another, then wealth, well-being, and success will also come. Only when everyone vows to become a loving, compassionate global citizen and employ a broad, international vision that sees all living beings as one will we all have tolerance and respect for one another. This is the only way we can all prosper, and the only way that the world will be filled with happiness and joy. When love is elevated to a higher level it is loving kindness and compassion, and these qualities *are* the Dharma; and where there is the Dharma, there is a Way.

When everyone does good deeds, speaks good words, and keeps good thoughts, then the love and compassion within the mind gains the power to eliminate negative karma.

Eliminating negative karma, however, will be an ongoing constant process until we find a truly sustainable happiness. In Buddhism, loving kindness and compassion are critically important, but this cultivation is only like one wing of a bird. For the bird to take off and soar, it also needs the wing of wisdom.

Buddhist wisdom is like a perfect, perpetual science. It is possible that all we now know about conventional science will one day be overturned, for science is ever changing. But the Dharma, the natural law of the universe, that the Buddha discovered and taught has always existed, and remains as fresh and new in our time as it has ever been, for the Dharma is universal and eternal.

Buddhism contains many profound concepts related to both the spiritual and material world, and as science has progressed it has gone further and further to validate the rationality and truthfulness of the Dharma. Though there have been great advances in medical science such that doctors can now transplant many vital organs, even the heart, science cannot substitute the intrinsic nature of the mind.

The technology to transform the mind is much more ancient, since countless generations have achieved peace of mind through meditation. However, if meditation is practiced without Buddhist wisdom alongside it, then one cannot break free of the cycle of birth and death. Such meditative practices as holding one's breath or opening chakras do not ultimately help us to reach a state of transcendence. People with these misconceptions are often trapped in these wrong types of meditation, as they develop the ability to maintain their concentration without also developing their wisdom. Such people can become obsessed with their meditative experiences, hurting themselves and the people around them. Having sincere faith in religion helps us to find meaning in life, but what if we place our faith in an unjust religion? Not only will it not uplift our spirit, but we will leave behind a legacy of confusion.

During the time of the Buddha there were many religious seekers who practiced various forms of asceticism with the hope that it would grant them great rewards in a future life. Some would fast, drink only water, or subsist only on fruit. Some would forego clothing, throw themselves in deep holes, lie on ice, walk through fire, or jump off cliffs. There were people who would chew on grass, eat filth, or sleep on thorns, dirt, leaves, or cow dung—but the practices did not lead these ascetics to discern the cause of suffering.

The pain they inflicted upon themselves in this life was for nothing, and they would be reborn to suffer yet again.

There are people who think that to have wealth and power is a sin. They could have good clothes, but would rather dress in rags. They could have good food, but would rather eat kitchen scraps that have spoiled. Some people only do so for honor and fame, and to demonstrate their moral superiority. Then there are those who become cynical because they feel their talents have not been admired. Instead of reflecting on the reasons that lead to such impediments, they criticize rich people who live in great mansions and earn enormous wealth as immoral and corrupt. This is the wrong idea, and should be corrected.

Both lust and aversion are forms of clinging, and lead to suffering. Liberation does not come either from suffering or happiness. Buddhism teaches the Middle Way; that we should be unmoved by feelings of suffering or happiness, love or hatred, and rid ourselves of our afflictions and attachments. In this way, we can attain true happiness.

Buddhism teaches that there are two truths: ultimate truth and relative truth. Relative truth varies depending on conditions; it is defiled, empty, impermanent, and brings suffering. Relative truth is not worth pursuing on a long-term basis. Ultimate truth is the world of nirvana: it is permanent, blissful, pure, and the true self. Ultimate truth is what we should take refuge in.

There are many figures throughout the Buddhist sutras who utter the phrase, "I am filled with Dharma joy, I detest worldly joy." The Dharma is the truth, and the happiness that comes from pursuing the truth is real and eternal. The happiness that comes from the Dharma arises from observing the five precepts, understanding cause and effect, and following the Middle Way. When we are filled with Dharma joy, we stay neither detached from nor attached to worldly desires. We neither avoid nor pursue worldly fame, we are at ease wherever we are, and we can find happiness now in this very moment. Only the Dharma can transport us beyond the harsh waves of life and death, delivering us to the other shore of eternal happiness.

This voyage is neither long nor short, and cannot be measured. The space outside of each individual stretches in all directions. Some of this space is more important to us than others, and the place that is most important is the one we call home. After a hard day's work we each hope to return to the warmth of our homes to recuperate our weary body and mind.

There have been countless conflicts over this space. Many wars, both ancient and modern, were fought over land, with each side vying for more space to call their own. But no matter how powerful and influential those kings, ministers, generals, and officials became, the land they were able to conquer was still limited. Even though modern science tells us that there are planets and stars as numerous as grains of sand in the Ganges River, it does not compare to the space within the mind.

The true mind is not born and does not die. It extends across the past, present, and future, without beginning or end. Its vastness stretches out in the ten directions, such that it is immeasurable, limitless, and infinite. If one can master the space within the mind, then the space outside the mind will be mastered as well, for absolute reality is nothing more than what exists within the mind. If we allow our minds to encompass the vastness of space, then we can become one with the universe such that there is no longer any difference between the self and others, nor any distinction between external and internal.

There is a saying in the Huayan School of Buddhism that "Each flower is a world, and each leaf is a Buddha." All is one and one is all. How can everything possibly be one? In Buddhism, one is not necessarily few and all is not necessarily many. For example, one flower, one speck of dust, one grain of sand, one world, and one universe are each "one" thing, yet they are of greatly different scope. Which is large and which is small? Most people will say that one universe is much larger than one flower, but this is not so. From the time a flower seed is planted in the ground until the time it sprouts and matures it has taken in the water from rainclouds, the nutrients of the fertilizer, light of the sun, and carbon dioxide from the air. All of the many causes that must combine together for the flower to grow are as vast as the universe, and thus the scope of a single flower and a single universe is not so different after all.

In Buddhism it is said that "all phenomena return to one," but if this is the case, where does this "one" return to? "One" returns to all phenomena. "One" is the essence of all phenomena, and all phenomena are forms of the "one." "One" and "all" are not two separate concepts, but share the same origin and development like two points on a circle.

This is similar to millions of people being able to watch a television program, even though there is only one person in a studio performing before a camera. Is this not a case of one being all? When one is all and all is one, time and space reach an extraordinary degree of unity and harmony. When this is understood we can then comprehend how non-duality is the true nature of all things. Then, we can directly experience how everything is produced through causes and conditions, and that there is very little distance and very little difference between "you" and "I." Everything in the world is connected to everything else so closely, we find ourselves face to face with all existence.

The universe, like everything within it, has arisen through dependent origination. The life of the universe is like a circle, without beginning or end, and nothing can be said about its origin or creation. The various Buddhist schools and sects each have their ideas—some say the universe arose through karma, some through a special kind of consciousness called the *alaya* consciousness, and others posit that the universe arose from a more absolute reality called the *dharmadhatu*. Regardless of their variance, all of these theories are tied to the fabrications of the mind. There is a phrase repeated often throughout the Buddhist sutras, "As the mind arises, so too do all phenomena." Without the mind, of what use would be all the Buddhist teachings? A single mind is capable of generating all phenomena, for the mind is capable of encompassing as many worlds as there are grains of sand in the Ganges River.

In many Buddhist temples the following verse is written:

> Mt. Sumeru* can contain a mustard seed;
> A mustard seed can conceal Mt. Sumeru.

Once, a scholar saw this verse and thought that it was very illogical, so he asked a nearby monastic, "Mt. Sumeru is supposedly very, very large, so it is not a problem for it to contain a mustard seed. But how can such a small thing as a mustard seed conceal something as large as Mt. Sumeru? This verse is too great of an exaggeration."

The monastic answered him, "Since you are a scholar, perhaps you have heard the Chinese expression, 'From reading books I have

---

* In Buddhist cosmology, Mount Sumeru is the tallest mountain in existence and is located at the center of the universe.

worn out ten thousand volumes; setting pen to paper, my thoughts are inspired.' Since a great scholar can contain ten thousand books, would you please swallow this book for me?"

The monastic handed the scholar a book, who looked at it in disbelief, "How can I swallow a book?"

"If you can stuff ten thousand books into your mind, why can't you put a single book into your stomach?"

Nothing can compare to the human mind in the greatness of its power and the swiftness of its thoughts. Where the material world has boundaries, the world of the mind is limitless. The mind can travel anywhere throughout the six realms of existence in a single thought.

The *Sutra on the Right Mindfulness of the True Dharma* says, "The mind is able to create all karma. It is because of the mind that there can be all karmic results." The sutra also describes the mind as a skillful painter, able to paint all things. The mind is a profound and unimaginable universe unto itself. Living beings may be reborn within the cycle of birth and death or they may have realized that the noble state of Buddhahood is all determined by the actions of the mind. But we will no longer need to seek anything outside of ourselves when we understand the immensity of the mind's abilities. When the mind has awakened, it will no longer fabricate delusions, and all of the mountains, rivers, trees, flowers, and every blade of grass will be contained within the mind. The thought of this present moment becomes the realm of absolute reality, and this world is instantly transformed into the Pure Land. All the phenomena of the universe that arise and cease within our consciousness become completely clear and known. This is awakening.

Awakening is the highest goal for most Buddhist practitioners. At the moment of awakening, the world of delusion shatters completely and another world manifests before us. Things that happened long ago will once more appear before our eyes, and people and events from the distant past will slowly gather around us. At the moment of awakening, the sense of time and space drop away, and everything is as it should be.

Awakening is very difficult to describe in words, for just as only the person who drinks a glass of water can know the degree to which it is hot or cold, only one who has awakened can truly know the state of awakening. Ordinarily, we only see life and this world by circling around it superficially, unable to penetrate what is inside. We know the way things are, but not *why* things are the way they are. After awakening, not only do we no longer see things in only a superficial way, but the profound mysteries of the universe become clear and evident in our minds, and everything becomes understood with no need for words.

Only by awakening the consciousness of all people as a whole can we completely transform our collective karma and sustainably improve social mores. Besides religion, any resolution to social problems requires the strengthening of our social education, an improvement of professional ethics, the upholding of truth and justice, and the elevation of civil rights. Each and every one of these aspects demands immediate attention.

The world has progressed from the period of the divine right of kings into the age of democratic rights, but this is not the end. The next great change is for the right to live to be promoted for all living beings. As this era approaches, all abusive behavior towards animals, such as overburdening horses and oxen with heavy loads and the hanging of live ducks and chickens upside down in the market must come to an end. The light of this society can only be made manifest through the advocacy of compassion and loving kindness for all beings, all the time. Come what may, Buddhism stands for the equality of all living beings, for it is only by treating all beings equally with this sense of loving kindness and compassion that the ultimate expression of human civilization can be achieved. This level of societal awakening would truly bring the Pure Land here, to this life.

Index of Texts

Venerable Master Hsing Yun extensively quotes the Buddhist sutras throughout his teachings, often sharing short passages from a staggering variety of works. If a reader is moved by a particular passage, the next step of visiting the literature itself can be a difficult one. An alphabetical list of sutras is provided below to assist in this process. The sutras are organized by their titles in English, except in such cases when the Sanskrit name of the text has become commonplace, as in the case of the *Dharmapada*. Each text is also listed with its Chinese title, both in Chinese characters and pinyin pronunciation.

Bei Sutra

    Bei Jing   孛經

Benevolent Kings Who Protect the Country Sutra

    Renwang Fuguo Jing   仁王護國經

Dharmapada

    Faju Jing   法句經

Dharmapada with Parables

    Faju Piyu Jing   法句譬喻經

Diamond Sutra

    Jingang Jing   金剛經

The Eight Realizations of a Bodhisattva Sutra

    Ba Daren Jue Jing   八大人覺經

Treatise on the Demonstration of Consciousness-Only

    Cheng Weishi Lun   成唯識論

Flower Adornment Sutra

    Da Fangguang Fo Huayan Jing   大方廣佛華嚴經

Sutra in Forty-two Sections

    Sishier Zhang Jing   四十二章經

Four-Part Vinaya

    Sifen Lu   四分律

Golden Light of the Ever-Victorious King Sutra

    Jinguangming Zuishengwang Jing   金光明最勝王經

Gratitude Sutra

    Baoen Jing   報恩經

Sutra of Illuminating Light

    Chuyao Jing   出曜經

Long Discourses of the Buddha

    Chang Ahan Jing   長阿含經

Lotus Sutra

    Fahua Jing   法華經

Sutra of Teachings Bequeathed by the Buddha

    Fo Yijao Jing   佛遺教經

Teachings to King Prasenajit Sutra

    Rulai Shijiao Shengjunwang Jing   如來示教勝軍王經

The Treasure Box Sutra

    Baoqie Jing   寶篋經

Sutra on the Upasaka Precepts

    Youpose Jie Jing   優婆塞戒經

Varsakara Sutra

    Yushi Jing   雨勢經

Non-Buddhist Classical Texts

The Analects of Confucius

    Lunyu   論語

The Essential Politics of the Zhenguan Era

    Zhenguan Zhengyao   貞觀政要

The History of the States

    Guoyu   國語

Records of the Grand Historian

    Shiji   史記

Glossary

(All dates are given in the common era, unless noted.)

Ajatasatru, King: King of Magadha at the time of the Buddha. He ascended the throne by killing his father, King Bimbisara. He later reformed and became a major supporter of Buddhism.

Amitabha Buddha: The Buddha of boundless light and boundless life. Amitabha is one of the most popular Buddhas for devotion among Mahayana Buddhists. He presides over the Pure Land of Ultimate Bliss.

Ananda: One of the ten great disciples of the Buddha, and the Buddha's cousin. He was the Buddha's attendant and known for his excellent memory.

Asoka, King: (r. 272-236 B.C.E) King of Maurya. His kingdom stretched over the majority of what is now India, and beyond into modern day Iran and Bangladesh. He sponsored many Buddhist missionaries and became a great patron of Buddhism.

Avalokitesvara Bodhisattva: The Bodhisattva of compassion, whose name in Sanskrit means "He who hears the cries of the world." Known as one of the great bodhisattvas of Mahayana Buddhism, and very popular throughout China. The "Universal Gate" chapter of the *Lotus Sutra* features him prominently.

Bhiksu: Title given to a male monastic disciple of the Buddha.

Bhiksuni: Title give to a female monastic disciple of the Buddha.

Bimbisara, King: King of Magadha at the time of the Buddha, later killed and usurped by his son Ajatasatru. He was a major supporter of Buddhism, and frequently invited the Buddha to teach in his capital city of Rajagrha.

Buddha: Sanskrit for "awakened one." Though there are many Buddhas, the term typically refers to Sakyamuni Buddha, the historical Buddha, and founder of Buddhism.

Buddha nature: The capacity to become a Buddha that is inherent to all living beings.

Buddha's Light International Organization: A lay Buddhist organization founded in 1992 by Venerable Master Hsing Yun. With chapters all over the world, the BLIA works to promote Buddhism, education, culture, and community service.

Cao Cao: (155-220) Chinese general, and later chancellor, known for his treachery.

Caste: Category of strict social division in ancient India. The Indian caste system of the Buddha's time features four castes:

brahman for brahmanical priests, *ksatriya* for warriors and kings, *vaisya* for merchants, and *sudra* for manual laborers. The Buddha opposed the caste system.

Causes and conditions: Commonly used to analyze causal relationships in a Buddhist context. In this form of analysis, a cause denotes the major factor which produces an effect. A condition is a factor which presence allows for a cause to produce a given effect. In the cause and effect phenomena of the growth of a plant, the seed is the cause, the sprouting of the seed is the effect, and factors such as the soil, sunlight, and water are the necessary conditions.

CCP: Chinese Communist Party.

Confucius: (551-479 B.C.E.) Early Chinese moral philosopher and founder of Confucianism; a philosophy which prizes education, order, responsibility, and filial piety.

Dependent origination: The Buddhist concept that all phenomena arise due to causes and conditions. The term is also sometimes used to specifically refer to the chain of causes that result in suffering, sickness, and death.

Desinicization: Taiwanese political movement that emerged at the turn of the twenty-first century and proposed that Taiwan should develop its own cultural identity separate from China.

Devadatta: A monastic disciple and cousin of the Buddha who wished to wrest leadership of the sangha away from the Buddha. He attempted to murder the Buddha several times.

Dharma: Sanskrit for "Truth." This can refer to the Buddha's teachings, as well as the truth of the universe.

Dharma realm: The true nature of our world, as seen without defilement or affliction. May also refer to a cosmological scheme which includes the six realms of existence [see *realm*], plus the realms of sravakas, pratyekabuddhas, bodhisattvas, and Buddhas.

Dharmakaya: One of the three "bodies" of the Buddha. The Dharmakaya is the aspect of the Buddha that is present throughout all of existence.

Dharmaraksa: One of the first Buddhist monastics to come to China. Produced the first Chinese translations of the sutras together with Kasyapa-matanga.

Duskrta: A category of monastic rules that are considered slight misdeeds. A monastic who has broken these rules can restore his or her standing through confession and repentance.

Eightfold path, noble: The path leading to awakening taught by the Buddha. Its eight factors are: (1) right view, (2) right thought, (3) right speech, (4) right action, (5) right livelihood, (6) right effort, (7) right mindfulness, and (8) right meditative concentration.

Five precepts: The most fundamental set of Buddhist precepts observed by lay and monastic Buddhists alike. They are (1) to refrain from killing, (2) to refrain from stealing, (3) to refrain from sexual misconduct, (4) to refrain from lying, (5) to refrain from consuming intoxicants.

Fo Guang Shan: Monastery founded by Venerable Master Hsing Yun in 1967 in Kaohsiung, Taiwan. The term "Fo Guang Shan," meaning "Buddha's Light Mountain," is also used to refer to the association of over two hundred branch temples around the world, and the many monastics ordained by Master Hsing Yun.

Fourfold assembly: The collective name for male Buddhist monastics, female Buddhist monastics, male lay Buddhists, and female lay Buddhists.

Ganges River: Indian river of great religious significance. In Buddhism, it is frequently used as a simile to describe things which are immeasurably large.

Great elements, four: Earth, water, fire, and wind or, more broadly, physicality, liquidity, heat, and movement. According to Buddhism, the human body and all elements of the physical environment are formed of these four elements.

Huayan School: Chinese school of Buddhism which used the *Flower Adornment Sutra* as its principle text.

Humanistic Buddhism: Buddhism practiced in a way that is engaged with the world and life-affirming. Major tenets include the integration of Buddhism with life and the creation of a "Pure Land on Earth." Venerable Master Hsing Yun is a proponent of Humanistic Buddhism.

Impermanence: Buddhist principle asserting that all phenomena which arise due to causes and conditions will eventually change and cease.

Intrinsic nature: The fundamental essence of all living beings. [see *Buddha nature*]

Kaniska, King: (r. 127-151) King of the Kushan Empire, which is now modern day Afghanistan.

Karma: Literally "action," though much more commonly used to describe the entirety of the Buddhist view of cause and effect. The Buddha stated that the causes, conditions, and rebirth we encounter in the future are effects of our previous thoughts, words, and deeds.

Karmic connection: An affinity created between living beings that will cause them to interact in future lives in either positive or negative ways, depending on the connection formed between them.

Kasyapa-matanga: One of the first Buddhist monastics to come to China. Produced the first Chinese translations of the sutras together with Dharmaraksa.

KMT: Chinese Nationalist Party.

Kumarajiva: (344-413) Buddhist monk and a prolific sutra translator. Many of his sutra translations are still commonly chanted in the Buddhist liturgy today.

Mainland China: Commonly used to refer to the People's Republic of China.

Maitreya Bodhisattva: A bodhisattva who is currently residing in Tusita heaven, ready to take birth as the next Buddha of our world in the distant future.

Manjusri Bodhisattva: The Bodhisattva of wisdom.

Medicine Buddha: The Buddha of healing. The Medicine Buddha presides over the Eastern Pure Land of Lapis Lazuli.

Mencius: (372-289 B.C.E.) Early Confucian scholar and author of an eponymous collection of aphorisms.

Milinda, King: (r. 155~130 B.C.E.) Greek King of northern India. His conversation with the Buddhist monk Nagasena and his eventual conversion are detailed in the *Nagasena Sutra*.

Nirvana: A state of perfect tranquility that is the ultimate goal of Buddhist practice.

Parajika: A category of monastic rules that are considered grave violations, like murdering a human being. A monastic who has broken these rules is expelled from the sangha.

Phenomena: English translation of *dharma*, when it is used to refer to thoughts, sensations, and other units of reality.

Prajna: Sanskrit for "wisdom," though typically referring to a transcendent variety of wisdom that comes from seeing the true nature of reality.

Prasenajit, King: King of Kosala during the time of the Buddha, as well as a prominent supporter and lay disciple.

Precept: A rule of moral conduct set down by the Buddha to guide one's Buddhist practice. There are several sets of precepts, with the five precepts being the most basic and fundamental [see *five precepts*]. There are also a set of eight precepts for practitioners on retreat, ten precepts for novice monastics, as well as 250 and 348 precepts respectively for male and female monastics.

Pure Land: A transcendent realm created through the power of a Buddha's vow to help end the suffering of its living beings, should they choose to be reborn there.

Qixia Temple: Chinese Buddhist temple located near Nanjing, in Jiangsu Province. Also the training monastery of Venerable Master Hsing Yun.

Realm: Used variously to describe several different Buddhist cosmological schemes. The "six realms of existence" refers to possible destinations of rebirth, and includes heaven, the asura realm, the human realm, the animal realm, the ghostly realm, and hell. The "three realms" includes the desire realm, the form realm, and the formless realm, and corresponds both to destinations of rebirth and meditative attainment.

Sakyamuni Buddha: Siddartha Gotama, the historical Buddha and founder of the religion we know today. The name "Sakyamuni" means "Sage of the Sakyans," which was the name of the Buddha's clan.

Sangha: The Buddhist community. In a broad sense it includes both monastics and laypeople, though most often it refers only to monastics.

Siladitya, King: (r. 606-646) Indian king and patron of Buddhism, written about in Xuanzang's record of his pilgrimage.

Skanda: In Buddhist cosmology, one of the generals under the deva king of the south. He is a guardian of Buddhist temples, and statues of his fierce visage are often found in Chinese Buddhist temples.

Sun Yat-sen, Dr.: (1866-1925) Chinese politician and revolutionary whose political philosophy has had great influence in both Mainland China and Taiwan.

Sutra: A Sanskrit word used to describe a variety of religious and non-religious writings, but most commonly used in a Buddhist context to refer to the recorded discourses of the Buddha.

Taizong, Emperor: (r. 627-649) Chinese emperor who presided over a great period of prosperity in China's history.

Treatise: A category of Buddhist religious texts which includes commentaries, expositions, manuals, and various other post-canonical Buddhist literature.

Vajra: A symbol of the indestructible. Commonly translated as "diamond" or "adamantine."

Vimalakirti: A lay bodhisattva who lived during the time of the Buddha. The *Vimalakirti Sutra* offers extensive teachings on non-duality.

Vinaya: The rules and regulations for Buddhist monastics.

Way: The Buddhist path of practice. May also refer more generally to a mode of conduct and discipline specific to a class of people (Ex. "The way of a king").

Xuanzang: (602-664) Prolific Chinese Buddhist translator who traveled to India to recover Buddhist sutras. The events of his pilgrimage were fictionalized into the classic Chinese novel *Journey to the West*.

Yao Xing, Emperor: (r. 394-416) First Chinese emperor to officially promote Buddhism as a state religion, and one of its greatest patrons.

Yogacara: Sanskrit for "practice of yoga," but commonly used to refer to the "Consciousness-Only" School of Buddhist psychology.

Zengzi: (504-436 B.C.E.) Student and contemporary of Confucius known for his filial piety.

Zhenguan era: (627-649) The imperial era name for the reign of Emperor Taizong of the Tang dynasty. Known as a golden age of Chinese history.

About Buddha's Light Publishing

Buddha's Light Publishing offers quality translations of classical Buddhist texts as well as works by contemporary Buddhist teachers and scholars. We embrace Humanistic Buddhism, and promote Buddhist writing which is accessible, community-oriented, and relevant to daily life.

Founded in 1996 by Venerable Master Hsing Yun as the Fo Guang Shan International Translation Center, Buddha's Light Publishing seeks to continue Master Hsing Yun's goal of promoting the Buddha's teachings by fostering writing, art, and culture. Learn more by visiting www.blpusa.com.